Lost Seasons

Lost Seasons

ARRESTS, SUSPENSIONS, CAREER
CHAOS, AND MORTALITY
AMONG NATIONAL FOOTBALL
LEAGUE (NFL) PLAYERS

• • •

Jeffrey S. Markowitz, Dr.P.H.

ISBN-13: 9780692597729
ISBN-10: 0692597727
Library of Congress Control Number: 2015921421
Jeffrey S. Markowitz, Princeton Junction, NJ

Contents

List of Tables

• • •

Prologue

• • •

I'D LIKE TO MAKE TWO things clear before starting: First, I love football and have since I was a young kid growing up in Brooklyn during the 1950s. Second, when I say "football," I mean American football, not soccer. My specific interest is in the players of the National Football League (NFL).

Many football books focus on elements of the game such as its rich history, its star players and coaches, its tactics and strategies, and its records and statistics. This book is different—instead of dealing with the game of football, it deals with the "game of life" among NFL players. In the game of football, there are goalposts, end zones, yard markers, gridlines, touchdowns, field goals, extra points, and many other things specific to the game. In the game of life for football players, there are lawyers, judges, court orders, suspensions, cut notices, and health and injury issues, to name just a few. The game of life is far more than just a game. The game of football, especially at the professional level, is also much more than a game.

These two "games," however, are not independent. In fact, the game of football and the game of life among its players may be very interrelated. For example, there are players who use performance-enhancing drugs (PEDs) in the hope of improving their performance on the field, and there are individuals who use illicit drugs to cope with the stress associated with playing in one of the most competitive leagues in the world. In these hypothetical examples, as well as dozens of real-life situations, there is overlap between on- and off-field activities. Certainly, this is also the case in other work settings. However, few workplaces engender the violence that's a big part of every NFL game. I sometimes wonder how difficult it must be to leave the football field and be able to completely turn off the violence.

In its earlier days especially, the NFL was mainly focused on improving the elements of the game and on the economic growth and survival of the league and individual teams. In recent decades, however, the NFL has been forced to shift some of its focus to game-of-life issues. There are aspects of the game that may cause havoc for the players in later life, and the league must own up to its responsibilities in this regard. For example, it's impossible to ignore on-field head injuries that may, later in life, lead to dementia, chronic traumatic encephalopathy (CTE), and other horrible neurodegenerative diseases.

Both the game of football and the game of life for football players can lead to "lost seasons." A lost season is not necessarily a season of the year or a season during a football year. What I'm referring to is a lost season in its broadest sense. It can occur over a period of days or years. Missed games, seasons, and shortened careers are definitely part of the scenario. So are court appearances, chronic pain, disabilities, and months or years lost later in life. In the game of football, injuries and performance issues are generally at the root of what I'm calling lost seasons. In the game of life of the sport, arrests, suspensions, and even mortality can come into play.

You do not need to be a football player, any kind of professional or non-professional athlete, or even an athlete at all to experience what I'm calling lost seasons. I remember that after finishing undergraduate school, when I was trying to figure out what I wanted to do as a career, I stumbled in and out of odd jobs, drank booze most nights, and generally didn't accomplish anything. This was a lost season for me that lasted several years. Most of us have experienced lost seasons of one kind or another during our lives, even though few of us live the demanding, grueling, violent lives that professional football players do.

In brief, the term "lost seasons" refers to any kind of lost time: a season- or career-ending injury; a DUI arrest with jail time; a shortened

NFL career due to performance; or even a curtailed life related to one's race, birthplace, or body size.

Most people would not consider arrests, suspensions, career loss, and mortality to be related in any way, and statistically, it could be difficult to make a connection. The players who get arrested, on average, may not be the same individuals who get league suspensions or who die at younger ages than their peers. But to the extent that these incidents and events engender some kind of loss for affected individuals or groups, they do share something in common.

Most other writing produced about the subjects covered in this book is not based on research or empirical data. Sports and Internet writers often report on a single incident, like a player getting arrested. What were the circumstances? How will this event impact the player involved, his team, and the league? This type of information can be useful to readers. However, these types of stories generally do not look at *trends* among groups of players. Are certain groups of players more likely to be involved in certain types of off-field incidents? Are more or fewer of these types of events occurring over time? These are the kinds of questions this book addresses in a scientific manner using the best data available.

I have taken care to provide the highest-quality data for all of the analyses contained in this book. However, with so much data involved, and so many steps in the research process, errors can occur. Every effort has been made to minimize errors.

I hope you enjoy reading this book as much as I relished working on it. If you have any comments, questions, or suggestions, please feel free to contact me by e-mail at jeffmarkowitz.lostseasons@gmail.com. Also, if you're interested in reading this book but can't afford to buy it, drop me a line, and I'll mail a copy to you.

CHAPTER 1

About the Data Collected for This Book

• • •

IT WAS APRIL 22, 2010, Earth Day, and large numbers of people from about 190 countries were participating in "A Billion Acts of Green," the theme for the highly anticipated events commemorating the fortieth anniversary of this day. There were Green-related celebrations, concerts, and special activities everywhere, like the World People's Conference on Climate Change in Bolivia and a large concert at the Washington Mall featuring stars like Sting, John Legend, Jimmy Cliff, and Joss Stone, to name just a few.

Another important event was taking place that night that had nothing at all to do with Earth Day. Coincidentally, it was the first day of the seventy-fifth NFL Draft. In addition to the thousands of excited fans packing Radio City Music Hall, a record-breaking seven-million-plus people would be watching the draft on either ESPN or the NFL Network. Yes, it was Earth Day 2010, but many NFL fans, including me, didn't even know that. The 2010 NFL Draft would undoubtedly be a life-changing event for many of the players selected. For me, it was the start of an exciting new research project that has culminated in the writing of this book.

It's easy to say now, in 2016, that the 2010 NFL Draft featured some very "special" players like Ndamukong Suh, Tim Tebow, Jahvid Best, Dez Bryant, Chris Cook, Trent Williams, Sean Weatherspoon, and Aaron Hernandez. (This is the last time I will mention players' names in this book. I'll explain why soon.) Many of the 2010 draftees have gone on to become stars in the NFL and earn millions of dollars. However, some of these players have gotten into trouble with the league and/or the law. Still others have suffered serious injuries that have interrupted, or completely ended, their careers.

I became intrigued with some of the players who were drafted in 2010 and began looking into their college-playing careers. It was amazing for me to see how much background and statistical information was available online on every draftee, and there were even more data on all current and former NFL players. Undoubtedly, the growth of fantasy football, now a multibillion-dollar industry in the United States (Goff 2013), fostered by the evolution and growth of the Internet, (Internet Society n.d.) played a vital role in the NFL information explosion.

In 2010, I was about to retire from a career as a health researcher. I had some knowledge of epidemiology, biostatistics, and outcomes research and did some computer programming. My training in these areas began during the 1980s as a graduate student at the School of Public Health at Columbia University in New York City. I was a lifelong football fan and began to think about ways of using my research skills to follow the players who were drafted in 2010. So it's not at all random that several of the chapters in this book deal specifically with the 2010 draftees.

Initially, I was mainly interested in collecting data on concussions. It didn't take long to discover the NFL website (www.nfl.com), where I found a treasure trove of data containing team rosters, game logs, injury reports, and player transactions. (NFL 2010–2014) For example, the online team rosters had the names, dates of birth, weights, heights, teams, positions, and several other bits of information about the players. I could use these data as background variables for descriptive purposes and also to examine possible risk factors for concussions.

Injury data, available in NFL injury reports, are published weekly during the football season. Name, type of injury, and game status for affected players are included. Longer-term, and more serious, injuries that result in players being placed on the league's Injured Reserve List

(IRL) are published on the "Transaction" pages on the NFL and ESPN websites.

Following the 2010 draftees through the subsequent years to determine the incidence of concussions was an exciting research idea because these players shared a common starting point in the NFL and were roughly the same age. While some 2010 draftees may have suffered head injuries prior to initiating their NFL careers, they all had "fresh starts" within the league, at least then, in 2010. Unfortunately, a sample of 255 players—the number of athletes selected in the 2010 NFL Draft—was probably too small to effectively study a somewhat rare injury like concussions. For this reason, I decided to expand my database to include all 2010 regular-season players. This would increase my sample size to more than 1,900 players, and I would be able to compute 2010 concussion incidence rates, as well as risk factors, for the entire league. Nevertheless, a year's worth of data, while a good start, would not be enough to look at trends over time.

During the next two years, 2011 and 2012, I collected more of the same type of data. By 2013, with three years of data in hand on every NFL regular-season player, I conducted extensive statistical analyses and wrote my first book, *Pigskin Crossroads: The Epidemiology of Concussions in the NFL, 2010–12* (Markowitz and Markowitz 2013). The data I had collected contained information on more than 5,700 player seasons, and there were several dozen variables on each individual in the database.

Writing *Pigskin Crossroads* turned out to be one of the most challenging yet rewarding things I've ever done. Even though my daughter and coauthor, Ariana, helped me a great deal, the writing itself was difficult, but it paled in comparison to the data collection, organization, and analysis. Yes, all of the data were available online, but it's not as if I could simply press a Download button and the data would appear ready for statistical analysis. In some cases, I had to copy and paste several rows of data at a time into a database.

This book contains empirical analyses, often based on five years of NFL data, from 2010 to 2014, and my interests have extended far beyond concussions. If you would like to gain insight into the kinds of analyses I've been able to produce with the football-related data I've collected, take a look at table 1-1. This table contains summary statistics for about a half dozen variables on every regular season player between 2010 and 2014. Several chapters in this book analyze NFL players for much longer periods of time. For example, the chapter on domestic violence covers a fifteen-year period, and the mortality chapter examines more than 7,700 players in the NFL cohort who played in the league during a twenty-seven-year period, between 1960 and 1986.

The "exposure" data used for some chapters in this book, adapted from NFL game logs, indicates each game that every player participated in between 2010 and 2014. I used the number of player games as the denominator for the incidence rates I calculated. These data could also be used to determine missed games, or even seasons, following injuries. With more than 1,900 players per season, after five years of data collection, there are now about 115,000 rows of exposure data alone. There are also now more than 23,000 rows of injury-report data that include every injury type (not just concussions), plus about 3,600 rows of player background data and hundreds of rows of IRL data.

I also computed new variables from the existing ones. For example, I used a player's date of birth to compute his age at the start of each regular season. I used the player's position to determine whether he played offense, defense, or kicked. From the exposure data, I was able to determine the number of seasons each individual had played and whether his NFL career had continued or ended. I used a player's height and weight to determine his body mass index.

To address the types of questions covered in my research, I often had to integrate, or "merge," the different types of data (e.g., background, injury, exposure). For the first two years of data collection, I attempted to do this based solely on players' names, which proved to be a big mistake. The variables used to merge two or more databases have to match exactly; using the names just doesn't work. This is because some players have the same names as other players, use both short and long versions of their own names, use nicknames, or in rare instances, completely change their names over time. The Injury Report database, for example, lists players' real names, while other databases use shortened names and nicknames. Without a consistent name among study years, or among the various databases, it is impossible to manage and organize the collected data effectively. After the 2011 season, I thought of a simple idea to resolve this problem: I would assign a unique identification number (ID) to each player. To separate two or more players with the same first and last names, I used their team and position to identify them. After five years of data collection, I have now assigned about 3,600 unique ID numbers. (This doesn't count the 7,700+ players included in the mortality database.)

Using ID numbers based on players' names also enabled me to add other kinds of data to my growing database. I've had an interest in social issues, including crime and arrests, since my undergraduate years at Queens College in New York, where I majored in political science and minored in sociology. In 2012, I discovered two online databases that publish arrest data on NFL players going back to 2000: the *USA Today* and *San Diego Union-Tribune* NFL arrest databases (*USA Today* 2000-14; *San Diego Union-Tribune* 2000-14).

I had total confidence in the validity and completeness of the data from the NFL website I was using for my research; the exact-same data appeared on the ESPN website (ESPN 2010-14) and several of the fantasy football websites. However, I had no experience using either of the arrest databases, so I conducted extensive checks to ensure that they were complete and accurate. For the large majority of arrests, the two online arrest databases contained similar or identical information, and this consistency was a good sign. In the rare cases when there was a discrepancy between the two arrest databases, I consulted other reliable news sources to make decisions. I also double-checked many of the arrest reports that appeared in the *USA Today* and *San Diego Union-Tribune* databases against published stories and was able to confirm the occurrence of virtually all of these reports.

Another data source I discovered in 2013 was the Spotrac database for NFL fines and suspensions (Spotrac 2002-14). Currently, this database goes back to 2002 and provides the type of offense committed by each player and the dollar amount for each fine and suspension. The number of games is given for the suspensions. I have also conducted extensive checks with this database and have yet to find an issue with the actual occurrence of any of the fines or suspensions. In just a few cases, however, there seemed to be some inconsistencies in the fine amounts and length of the suspensions that appeared. This is probably due to the fines-and-suspension appeals process for NFL players and possible changes in the length of suspensions and the monetary amounts forfeited as a result.

Once I added my ID numbers to the players' names listed in the online arrest and fines-and-suspensions databases, I could easily integrate the data from these databases with the background, injury, exposure, and arrest data. The end product is a completely novel, five-year longitudinal database containing a wealth of interesting information that I used to address a wide range of important empirical research questions about NFL players. This book represents the fruits of this effort.

In mid-2015, as I was writing this book, I discovered several new variables and data sources. In the Stats section of the NFL website, there is a Player tab. Every current and former or "historic" player who ever played in the NFL can be found here. As part of each player's vital information, like height, weight, and years played, this page indicates whether a player is alive or dead. As it turned out, this same information is also available at Pro-Football Reference.com. In addition to indicating which players have died, the website provides the date of death. The mortality and longevity of NFL players is obviously a critical subject, and I examine several questions related to them in this book. Just to be clear, this is off-the field mortality that generally occurs years or even decades after players retire. Although several studies on this subject do exist, they have limitations.

I mentioned earlier that I would not include players' names in the rest of this book. Certainly, reports on NFL players, particularly when they are injured or get into trouble with the law or the league, are not private matters. Fantasy football fans and (legal) gamblers, in particular, are hungry to learn as much as possible about players' ability to play and factors that might interfere with them doing so. The league itself publishes reports on all suspensions and injuries and players' game status (NFL, Injury Reports 2010-14).

Epidemiologists care about the individuals they study. However, most or all of the analyses they conduct are based on aggregated groups; individuals are generally not identified. With HIPAA, the federal Health Insurance Portability and Accountability Act of 1996, (US Department of Health and Human Services 1996) and local institutional review board (IRB) requirements, there are strict rules governing the privacy, confidentiality, and use of names in health research.

Given the very public nature of NFL player information, I don't believe I would be breaking any laws if I used players' names in this book. I did, however, conduct empirical research, combine data from diverse sources, and analyze the data in ways that have never been done before. I could, for example, write that a specific NFL player had fines for late hits, had suspensions for substance abuse, suffered multiple concussions, and had arrests for domestic violence. Certainly, it is not my intent to embarrass, expose, or hurt any player's reputation or career. Moreover, it would not add in any way to the quality of my research to report any players' names. There are several instances in which I present anonymous case histories of players and describe certain actions or injuries. It is possible that a knowledgeable reader could recognize one or more of the players being reported based on this information. Also, some reference citations contain players' names. However, this is as far as I go with respect to players' names. I refrained from naming players in my first book, and for the reasons I just described, I continued that policy for this book.

This book focuses on NFL regular-season players. I excluded players on preseason rosters who never played in a regular season. I did this for a number of important research and practical reasons that I will detail later in the book. Briefly, focusing on regular-season players facilitates denominator calculations used to compute incidence rates and reduces the amount of data that has to be collected and managed.

I conducted statistical tests for this book. However, I've attempted to keep them to a minimum and have put most of the detailed statistical information in the tables rather than the text. The reason, briefly, is that the more tests that are conducted, the greater is the likelihood of reporting differences that do not really exist. This is because each test carries with it some likelihood of providing false positive results, and this probability increases with each test that's performed. Nevertheless, given the number of statistical tests I conducted for this book, there are likely to be several false-positive findings, and readers should keep this in mind.

Readers who never studied statistics may not understand exactly what I have done with the data in every instance. In some sentences, I have attempted to explain a statistical concept or test. I suggest that you refer to the table displays while you read each chapter. This will help you see trends that should improve your understanding of the data and the results.

As you'll see, all of the tables in this book are shown at the end of each chapter after the respective Reference sections.

Please keep in mind that I conducted the statistical tests presented in this book to detect *differences*. When I report that something is "significant," it means a difference exists that is unlikely to be attributable to chance alone. In some instances, I have reported p-values. The smaller the p-value (shown in the table displays), the less likely it is that the given result is due to chance. For purposes of this book, any p-value less than or equal to 0.05 is considered statistically significant, suggesting that a difference exists. In some instances, a sample size could reduce the likelihood of uncovering significant statistical results. Caution is therefore required, especially when interpreting nonsignificant results involving smaller numbers.

In this book, I cite a plethora of data, information, and articles that appear on the Internet. However, these are not all "created equal." Journal papers published in the biomedical literature usually go through a peer-review process. The same generally cannot be said for Internet articles. In addition, the goals and objectives of these two types of publications can be quite different. The differences between these two types of articles do not ensure the quality or credibility of one over the other. Unfortunately, however, and with few exceptions, there are *not* a lot of scientific journal articles on many of the topics covered in this book. Although extensive social science literature has been published in journals on topics like domestic violence, driving under the influence, and substance abuse, little of this information applies specifically to NFL players.

I have cited Internet articles within this book to present certain viewpoints or, when possible, to support or reject selected ideas. In several instances, I critique specific articles on the web. I believe that citing Internet reports in a scientific book like this requires special caution. There is a need to discern facts and truth from beliefs and feelings and to distinguish real data from biased or inaccurate reports. The scientific literature must also be scrutinized. In any case, it is my belief that the Internet contains usable data, citable reports, and information that is worth including in a book like this.

The next nine chapters of this book are all based on original empirical research I conducted using the data previously described. The specific methods used in each study are detailed within each chapter. The nine chapters are divided into four parts:

1. Arrests
2. Suspensions and Fines
3. Career Chaos
4. Mortality

Here is a brief description of the content of these sections.

ARRESTS

There are four chapters related to arrests among NFL players. Chapter 2 identifies every arrest of regular-season NFL players that took place between 2010 and 2014. I divided these arrests into violent and nonviolent crimes. I calculated the arrest rates for each of these two types of crimes and identified the risk factors.

Several recent high-profile domestic-violence cases involving NFL players have brought more attention to this very serious problem. Little is known, however, about the epidemiology of domestic-violence arrest rates among NFL players. I identified all domestic-violence arrests of regular-season NFL players during a fifteen-year study period, from 2000 to 2014. Chapter 3 provides the domestic-violence arrest rates for NFL players for each of these years and for all fifteen years combined and also identifies trends over time. I analyzed variables like team, position, and the time of year that the domestic-violence arrests occurred.

Driving under the influence (DUI) is another serious public health problem that has impacted a number of NFL players. Like domestic violence, DUI is obviously an issue that affects the general population as well. When NFL players are arrested for DUI, these events sometimes receive a great deal of publicity, and some Internet sports writers have pointed to an "out-of-control" problem among NFL players. Chapter 4 compares DUI arrest rates among NFL players with the general population for a four-year study period, 2010–13. Age-specific analyses address the question of whether rates of DUI arrests are different between NFL players and similarly aged men in the general population. The results may surprise you.

Between 2010 and 2014, a growing number of underclassmen were drafted into the NFL. These individuals were often drafted in early rounds, and given their young ages and notoriety, these underclassmen may be more likely to have off-field issues, including arrests. Chapter 5 examines the arrest rates of drafted NFL underclassmen versus a sample of nonunderclassmen controls. I matched the two groups of NFL players according to the year they were drafted and the place they were selected in their respective drafts. I compared the arrest types and numbers for these two groups of players.

Suspensions/Physical Fines

Chapters 6 and 7 describe the respective epidemiologies of suspensions and physical fines in the NFL between 2010 and 2014. The large majority of suspensions in the NFL are for substance abuse and the use of performance-enhancing drugs (PEDs). In some instances, suspensions can cost players tens of thousands of dollars in lost salaries and may also place players' careers in jeopardy. Very little is actually known about suspensions in the NFL, as far as who gets them, their numbers each year, their length, and the amount of money that suspended players forfeit.

Many fines given out by the NFL are for offenses that are not physical in nature. Some of these, like texting during a game or throwing a ball into the stands, may be pretty trivial. Some of the other offenses that get fined by the league, like hits to the head, late hits, and even physical contact with a referee, though, can be quite serious and endangering to affected individuals. Chapter 7 focuses solely on these kinds of physical fines and describes how often they occur and the characteristics of the perpetrators. NFL salaries can be quite high, and fines for physical offenses that seem like a lot to the average person can represent just a small fraction of the NFL player's compensation. Chapter 7 also describes inconsistencies in the way the NFL metes out suspensions and fines.

Career Chaos

There is quite a bit of career chaos in the NFL. Short or disrupted careers may be due to, for example, off-field issues, injuries, and "marginal" playing performance (relative to other world-class athletes). IRL injuries are among the most serious that NFL players experience. As a rule, individuals placed on the IRL during 2010 and 2011, could not return to playing in the NFL during the season of their respective injuries. In chapter 8, I compare the extent of careers terminated by players placed on the IRL during these years to the ending of careers of two groups of players who did not appear on the IRL. As far as I can tell, careers ending following placement on the IRL have never been studied before.

Chapter 9 follows the players selected in the 2010 NFL Draft for a five-year period to determine whether they have experienced several specific on- and off-field outcomes. All of these outcomes are directly related to the players' careers or have the potential to affect their careers. The three types of outcomes studied are specifically career related and include playing only one or two of the possible five seasons between 2010 and 2014, interrupted careers, and ended careers. The second outcome is simply called "trouble" and includes arrests, suspensions, and physical fines. The third type of outcome is injury related and includes concussions and IRL injuries. During the five-year study period, the large majority of 2010 NFL draftees had experienced one or more of these outcomes.

MORTALITY

Chapter 10 focuses on mortality resulting from all causes among a large cohort of more than 7,700 individuals who played in the NFL between 1960 and 1986. It is important to note, once again, that this study does not look at mortality that occurs on the playing field, which is virtually nonexistent in regular-season play in the NFL. I looked at NFL players living or dying years after their NFL careers have ended. I analyzed about half a dozen potential risk factors in relationship to players being alive or dead by the vital-status end date of August 10, 2015. This analysis includes age, playing time body mass index, race, position, birthplace, and number of seasons played in the league. Some of these variables have already emerged in the biomedical literature as risk factors for mortality in the general population and among NFL players as well. However, variables like birthplace and number of seasons played in the league have never been studied in this regard. Do disparities exist between certain groups of NFL players as far as the risk of death?

I know that some of the topics covered in this book may seem gloomy, or even dark, to some readers. My intent is not to bash the NFL or its players, or to present a one-sided view of things. Moreover, some of the results I've obtained are not intended to justify a negative view of the league or the players, as may be inferred. As a public health professional, I tried to uncover the facts using empirical data. My ultimate goal is to prevent the occurrence of many of the issues and problems that are presented in this book, including domestic violence, DUI, other types of arrests, and suspensions. In the case of mortality, the goals should be to extend the quality of lives and to eliminate disparities between key groups of players. Only by understanding these problems better and identifying which players are at risk can we begin to develop ways to reduce their incidence.

REFERENCES

ESPN. 2010-14. "NFL." http://espn.go.com/nfl/.

ESPN. "NFL Transactions." http://m.espn.go.com/nfl/transactions.

Goff, B. 2013. "The $70 Billion Fantasy Football Market." *Forbes*. http://www.forbes.com/sites/briangoff/2013/08/20/the-70-billion-fantasy-football-market/.

Internet Society. n.d. "Brief History of the Internet." http://www.internetsociety.org/internet/what-internet/history-internet/brief-history-internet.

Markowitz, J. S., and Markowitz, A. 2013. *Pigskin Crossroads: The Epidemiology of Concussions in the National Football League, 2010–12*. CreateSpace.

NFL. 2010–2014. http://www.nfl.com/.

Pro-Football Reference.com. "Search the Pro-Reference.com Football Encyclopedia of Pages." http://www.pro-football-reference.com/players/.

Spotrac. 2002-14. "NFL Fines and Suspensions." http://www.spotrac.com/nfl/fines-suspensions/.

San Diego Union-Tribune. 2000-14. "NFL Arrests Database." http://www.sandiegouniontribune.com/nfl/arrests-database/.

USA Today. 2000-14. "NFL Player Arrests." http://www.usatoday.com/sports/nfl/arrests/.

US Department of Health and Human Services. "The Health Insurance Portability and Accountability Act of 1996 (HIPPA) Privacy, Security and Breach Notification Rules." HHS.com. http://www.hhs.gov/ocr/privacy/.

Table 1-1. Description of NFL Players in Database by Season, 2010–14									
Season ===>	2010		2011		2012		2013		2014
	n=1,926		n=1,910		n=1,938		n=1,911		1,936
Age (in years)									
Mean (SD)	26.4 (3.5)		26.3 (3.4)		26.1 (3.3)		26.1 (3.2)		26.0 (3.2)
Median	26		26		25		25		25
Range	20 to 46		20 to 43		20 to 42		20 to 40		20 to 41
Height (in inches)									
Mean (SD)	73.9 (2.6)		73.9 (2.6)		73.9 (2.6)		73.8 (2.7)		73.9 (2.6)
Median	74		74		74		74		74
Range	66 to 81		65 to 81		64 to 81		64 to 81		64 to 81
Weight (in pounds)									
Mean (SD)	246.3 (45.3)		245.6 (45.2)		245.5 (45.5)		245.7 (45.6)		245.4 (45.4)
Median	240		240		240		240		240
Range	155 to 376		155 to 360		155 to 364		160 to 360		160 to 364
Six-Group Position	N	%	N	%	N	%	N	%	N	%
Offensive linemen	325	16.9%	327	17.1%	335	17.3%	315	16.5%	323	16.7%
Defensive linemen	298	15.5%	292	15.3%	293	15.1%	294	15.4%	296	15.3%
Offensive backs	251	13.0%	245	12.8%	247	12.8%	245	12.8%	243	12.6%
Defensive backs	655	34.0%	639	33.5%	651	33.6%	636	33.3%	656	33.9%
Receivers	319	16.6%	332	17.4%	339	17.5%	351	18.4%	346	17.9%
Kickers	78	4.1%	75	3.9%	73	3.8%	70	3.7%	72	3.7%

Part One
Arrests

• • •

CHAPTER 2

Arrests for Violent and Nonviolent Crimes

• • •

UNFORTUNATELY, BEING ARRESTED AND SERVING time in US jails are as American as apple pie. In the year 2012 alone, about 12.2 million arrests were made in the United States. Nearly three-fourths of all of these arrests were of males. According to one arrest-history survey based on self-reports, by the time Americans reach the age of twenty-three, about 30 percent have been arrested (Brame et al. 2014). Among males, these rates are much higher, averaging 49 percent in African Americans and about 40 percent in whites (Brame et al. 2014). A large percentage of all adult arrests in males in 2010, about 86 percent, were between eighteen and forty-four years of age (FBI 2010), the same age range encompassing virtually all NFL players. In 2013, more than 278,000 arrests, 4.6 percent of all arrests, in the United States were for violent crimes, including murder, rape, robbery, and aggravated assault (FBI 2013).

Arrests are not convictions, and in the United States, there is a presumption of innocence for all arrestees. Inevitably, however, some arrests do lead to convictions, and in some instances, jail time. In fact, the United States has the dubious distinction of having the largest prison population of any country in the world. Almost one out every four prisoners in the world are held in prisons throughout the United States (National Research Council 2014), and about 1 percent of all US adults are serving time in prison (National Research Council 2014). Moreover, evolving criminal justice policy in the United States has resulted in more time spent behind bars in recent years (The Pew Charitable Trusts 2012). According to one independent study, the average time spent in US jails has increased by nine months, or 36 percent, comparing prisoners released in 2009 to those released twenty years earlier (The Pew Charitable Trusts, 2012). Jail time associated with both violent and nonviolent crimes can be substantial due to mandatory sentencing policies and stricter guidelines than in the past. Between 1992 and 2002, for example, the average time served in federal prisons for drug offenses increased from about thirty-three to forty-three months (Sentencing Project n.d.).

For reasons related to poor education, low income, discrimination, biased policing, and numerous other factors, African Americans have arrest rates that exceed their numbers in the general population. In 2013, for example, the FBI in the United States reported more than nine million total arrests. More than 2.5 million of these arrests, about 28 percent, were among African Americans (FBI 2013). However, only 14 percent of the US population in 2014 was African American (BlackDemographics 2014). In fact, African Americans are overrepresented in the NFL relative to the greater US general population. According to several unofficial, yet consistent, reports (Powell-Morse 2014; Wikipedia 2015a; Heavy Sports 2014), about 68 percent of NFL players in 2014 were African American, easily exceeding the 14 percent US total population statistic previously referenced. Nevertheless, the impact of race on arrests among NFL players has not been well studied.

In general, there is limited scientific literature on arrests among NFL players. Internet articles on this subject express a view that arrests are pervasive and out of control (Amendola 2013). As one Internet sports writer puts it, "Player arrests are becoming to the NFL what steroids were to Major League Baseball: an out-of-control problem" (Amendola 2013). These articles often focus on violent situations among high-visibility individuals, such as the following:

1. The NFL player currently serving a life sentence (without the possibility of parole) for a 2013 murder in Massachusetts and awaiting trial for a separate double homicide

2. The NFL player who first killed his girlfriend and later himself in Kansas City

3. The NFL player who knocked out his fiancé in an Atlantic City casino elevator

4. The NFL player charged in Texas with beating his four-year-old son with a tree branch.

Sadly, many more violent cases involving NFL players could be added here.

All of these individual cases are very unfortunate, and it would be difficult to find anything positive to say about any of them. However, despite hundreds of Internet articles written about individual players, like the ones just described, very little has been written to add to our understanding of these problems. The existing Internet literature fails to quantify the actual scope of the problem of arrests among NFL players. In fact, not much scientific attention has been paid to this problem, either. Two distinguished researchers, Benedict and Klein (1997, 169), make reference to this lack of attention as it relates to athletes in general and sexual violence: "Although the subject of athletes and sexual aggression is regularly featured in the media, it is rarely seriously studied. Journalistic treatment of athletes and sexual assault has focused attention on the problem but done little to deepen our understanding of it."

Numerous articles have appeared in the Internet literature that use data from online arrest databases like *USA Today* and *San Diego Union-Tribune*. The information in virtually all of these reports, however, is flawed based on details like these:

- Absent or inappropriate denominators
- The numerator not being a subset of the denominator
- Failure to include meaningful comparison groups
- The absence of statistical testing

In fact, the Internet articles on this subject were written by individuals without epidemiological or biostatistics training. While their articles may be interesting and well-intended, the authors generally lack the scientific skills that these kinds of topics deserve and require.

This chapter discusses the epidemiology of arrests among NFL players. I examined the population of players who played in an NFL regular season during a five-year period, from 2010 to 2014, and calculated rates of arrest. I determined arrest rates for crimes that are violent versus nonviolent separately. I also conducted risk-factor analyses.

METHODS

Any player who participated in an NFL regular season between 2010 and 2014 is eligible to be included in this study. I excluded players who never played in the NFL or who played in one or more preseasons only. The eligible regular-season players serve as the denominator for the arrest rates that appear in this chapter.

I obtained arrest (numerator) data from both the *USA Today* and *San Diego Union-Tribune* arrest databases for NFL players (*USA Today* 2010-14, *San Diego Union-Tribune* 2010-14). In about 98 percent of instances, the arrest reports that appear in the two databases are identical. I double-checked the remaining arrests (*n* = 6) against reliable news sources to ensure that they did, in fact, occur. In all six instances, I readily confirmed the arrests. There is no clear-cut pattern to help explain why these arrests appear in only one of the arrest databases. One of the cases that appeared in the *USA Today* "NFL Player Arrests" database involved only the Kansas City Chiefs player who murdered his girlfriend and then killed himself on the same day. This player obviously committed a crime, but because of his subsequent suicide, he was never arrested. Perhaps this is why this incident is not counted as an arrest in one of the databases.

About 6 percent of all entries in the *USA Today* and *San Diego Union-Tribune* arrest databases during the study period contain more than one arrest type, with listings like "Assault, Alcohol" or "Burglary, Gun." I counted these arrests only once based on the primary charge that appears in the arrest databases.

I reviewed all arrests used in this study to ensure that the type of arrest noted in the online database actually matches its description. In several instances, the arrest type fails to accurately describe the crime that is alleged. An example of this is an arrest designated as "Handicapped parking," with the following description appearing in the *USA Today* database: "Accused of leaving the scene, reckless driving, and driving with a suspended license after being caught parking in handicap spot" (*USA Today* "NFL Player Arrests" database October 2014). I thus reclassified this arrest as "Reckless driving." In all, I made three changes to the published arrest type.

I categorized all arrests based on whether they involved violent or nonviolent acts. The National Institute of Justice (2014a) defines a violent crime as follows: "In a violent crime, a victim is harmed by or threatened with violence. Violent crimes include rape and sexual assault, robbery, assault, and murder" (National Institute of Justice 2014a). In effect, this definition of violent crimes includes arrests for offenses like domestic violence, assault, murder, child abuse, battery, sexual assault, and several others. (A complete list of violent crimes identified in this chapter is provided in the "Results" section of this chapter.) I counted any arrest with a violent aspect to it, whether for a primary or secondary charge, as a violent crime.

I did not automatically designate all alleged crimes with the same arrest type as violent or nonviolent crimes. Again, I used the description of the alleged crime rather than relying solely on the arrest type listed in the online databases. For example, almost all arrests designated as "Gun" indicate possession charges but feature no violent acts. However, I deemed one arrest for a "Gun" charge to be violent based on its description as follows: "Police near Dallas issued warrant accusing him [arrestee] of firing gun near head of sister's boyfriend" (*USA Today* 2011).

I provided frequency distributions of violent and nonviolent crimes. I did not calculate rates for each individual arrest type, mainly because of their small numbers. I computed arrest rates per thousand eligible regular-season players and broke them down by study year and violent versus non-violent arrests. I identified risk factors, evaluating the following variables: age, weight, position, team, year, and month of arrest. Month of arrest is aggregated into two categories: "Football-playing season" months are August through January, and "off-season" months are February to July.

I categorized players' field positions into six independent groups: offensive linemen (centers, offensive guards, and tackles), defensive linemen (defensive tackles, ends, and nose tackles), offensive backs (halfbacks, fullbacks, and quarterbacks), defensive backs (linebackers, cornerbacks, and safeties), receivers (wide receivers and tight ends), and kickers (punters and placekickers).

I identified risk factors for arrests of violent and nonviolent crimes separately using incidence rate ratios (IRRs) with 95 percent confidence intervals (95 percent CI). An IRR is simply the ratio of two incidence rates, or one incidence rate over another.

Here are details about the incidence rate ratio analyses presented in this chapter:

- Just as an example, if one incidence rate is three per thousand annually and a second rate is two per thousand annually, then the IRR is 3/2, or 1.5.
- The two incidence rates are significantly different from each other if the confidence interval excludes the number 1.
- To minimize the number of statistical tests performed, I assigned index reference groups for the study year (e.g., 2010), age (e.g., twenty-four years and younger), weight (e.g., 215 pounds and under), position (e.g., offensive linemen), and time of year (e.g., during the football playing season).
- I compared selected groups of players to these arbitrarily assigned index groups, and the statistics are based on these comparisons.

RESULTS

I identified a total of 267 arrests during the period from 2010 through 2014. Because twenty-six of these arrests failed to meet entry criteria for this study, I dropped them from all analyses. This includes arrests among seventeen players who never played in an NFL regular-season game and nine players who played in a regular season, but prior to the 2010 season. In the two arrest databases combined, 241 unique arrests were reported for regular-season players during the study period. These 241 arrests are the focus of the analyses presented in this chapter.

Arrest types for eligible players broken down by violent and nonviolent crimes are shown in table 2-1. These results are simple frequency distributions, not arrest rates. Of the 241 total arrests, 61 are for violent crimes, and 180 are for nonviolent ones. Domestic violence ($n = 23$) and assault ($n = 23$) are the most common violent crimes, representing a total of 69 percent of all such arrests. Driving under the influence (DUI) is easily the most common type of arrest for a nonviolent crime ($n = 63$), more than double the number of arrests for the next-most-common arrest type, drugs ($n = 30$).

As shown in table 2-2, the rate of nonviolent arrests in all study years except 2013 range from 17.1 to 18.1 arrests per 1,000 regular season players per year. In 2013, the nonviolent arrest rate spiked to 23.0 per 1,000 players. Rates of arrests for violent crimes generally increased over time, from 5.7 to 7.2 per 1,000 players in 2014. The year 2012 is an exception to this trend, with a violent crime arrest rate of 5.7 per 1,000 players. When combining all five study years, the rate of arrests for nonviolent and violent crimes is 18.7 and 6.3 per 1,000 players per year, respectively.

RISK FACTORS

A statistical summary of all risk-factor results for violent and nonviolent arrests is shown in table 2-3.

AGE

Arrests for nonviolent crimes vary significantly by age in an inverse manner. The following information can be derived. Arrest rates for nonviolent crimes decline with each older age group, ranging from 12.1, 18.7, and 24.1 arrests per 1,000 players aged twenty-eight years and older, twenty-five to twenty-seven years, and twenty-four years and younger, respectively. The difference in these nonviolent arrest rates between the youngest and the oldest age group is significant. This pattern of results does not hold for arrests for violent crimes, with the twenty-five- to twenty-seven-year-olds having the highest overall rates of 8.2 arrests per 1,000 players per year, the youngest age group having a 5.3, and the oldest a 5.5 rate. These differences are not statistically significant.

WEIGHT

For both nonviolent and violent crimes, arrest rates decline with each heavier weight group. For example, players who weigh 215 pounds or less average 20.5 nonviolent arrests per 1,000 players, compared to 19 and 16.7 arrests per 1,000 players weighing 216 to 259 pounds and 260 pounds or more, respectively. A similar pattern is obtained with respect to arrests for violent crimes, for which rates are 7.4 per 1,000 players in the lightest group and 6.3 and 5.3 in the next two heavier weight groups. None of these arrest-rate differences based on weight are statistically significant.

PLAYER POSITION

Position is a consistent and significant risk factor for both violent and nonviolent crimes. Specifically, compared to offensive linemen, several groups of players have significantly elevated rates of arrests. For violent crimes, this includes defensive linemen (IRR = 11.0), offensive backs (IRR = 9.2), and defensive backs (IRR = 18.1). Similarly, these same three position types, plus receivers, have significant nonviolent arrest-rate elevations when compared to offensive linemen. The IRRs for these four position types versus offensive linemen are 3.3, 3.4, 2.3, and 3.5, respectively. Kickers have only two arrests for nonviolent crimes during the entire five-year study period and are not significantly different from offensive linemen in terms of both violent and nonviolent arrests.

Time of Year

Arrests rates during football-playing months and off-season months are also shown in table 2-3. For these analyses, the overall numbers of arrests are combined across the five study years. July and February, both off-season months, have the most arrests ($n = 31$ and $n = 27$, respectively). As a point of comparison, none of the months during the pre- and regular seasons have more than seventeen total arrests (in January). Arrests for violent crimes are the highest in June and July ($n = 8$ each). July and February are highest for nonviolent-crime arrests ($n = 23$ and $n = 22$, respectively). When the months are collapsed into football-playing months and off-season months, 149 of the 241 arrests (61.8 percent) occur during the off-season, and 92 (38.2 percent) take place during the football-playing months, which is statistically significant (IRR = 1.64). While not significant, the same pattern of results is observed for violent crimes (IRR = 1.59). It can be derived that the incidence rate for nonviolent crimes is 64 percent higher during off-season months compared to football months, and 59 percent higher for violent crimes.

Team

The numbers of arrests for violent and nonviolent crimes and arrest rates broken down by team for all five study years combined is shown in table 2-4. Given that there are thirty-two NFL teams, most of these results are based on small numbers of arrests and need to be interpreted with caution. There is a fair amount of variability with respect to the number of arrests per team and arrest rates. The teams with the highest arrest rates for violent crimes include the Bengals (20.3 per 1,000 players per year), the Vikings (18.1 per 1,000 players per year), and the Broncos (17.7 per 1,000 players per year). The violent-crime arrest rates for these three teams are more than, or nearly three times, the rate of the entire league (6.3 per 1,000 players per year). Five teams have no violent-crime arrests for the five-year study period, including the Texans, the Bills, the Colts, the Giants, and the Jaguars.

With respect to nonviolent crime arrests, the highest rates were obtained by the Vikings (39.7 per 1,000 players per year); the Bucs (38.0 per 1,000 players per year); and the Broncos (35.5 per 1,000 players per year). As a point of comparison, the annualized average for the league as a whole for the five-year study period is 18.7 arrests for nonviolent crimes. Three teams have especially low arrest rates for nonviolent crimes: the Texans (0 per 1,000 players per year), the Panthers (3.2 per 1,000 players per year), and the Saints (3.4 per 1,000 players per year).

Post Hoc Analysis of Specific Player Positions

In light of the importance of player position type as a risk factor for both violent- and nonviolent-crime arrests, I looked more closely at these data in post hoc analyses. (This is a statistical analysis that wasn't originally planned and that I conducted after seeing other related results. Special caution is required when interpreting the results of post hoc analyses because other results have already been examined.) The initial analysis just presented aggregates players into six position groups. The post hoc analysis generates arrest rates for all available positions (see table 2-5). The positions with the highest rates of arrests for nonviolent crimes include fullbacks, defensive tackles, and halfbacks, which all average more than 30 arrests per 1,000 players per year. The positions with the highest arrest rates for violent crimes include linebackers, cornerbacks, and safeties. These three groups average about 12 or more violent crime arrests per 1,000 players per year, which is close to double the league average. Arrest rates for violent and nonviolent crimes are low for nose tackles, quarterbacks, offensive guards, centers, punters, and kickers.

Discussion

One disturbing trend uncovered in the data in this chapter is the small, nonsignificant, but steady increase in arrest rates for violent crimes among NFL players between 2010 and 2014. This is quite different from national trends that generally show a decline in arrests for violent crimes in the US general population during this same period of time. In 2010, for example, the FBI reported a total of more than 298,000 arrests for violent crimes in the United States among males aged eighteen years and older. This number dropped in each of the next three years, getting to about 288,000, 285,000, and just over 278,000 in each of the years.

Arrests for nonviolent crimes do not increase for each year of this study. However, the two years with the highest nonviolent crime arrest rates are the two most recent ones studied, 2013 and 2014. Clearly, there is no reduction in either violent or nonviolent arrest rates among NFL players over the five-year study period, and any existing efforts by the NFL aimed at minimizing this problem should be carefully scrutinized. The NFL's Personal Conduct Policy, modified in 2014 (NFL 2014) following an NFL arrest scandal, requires an evaluation of its effectiveness in terms of reducing the number of arrests among NFL players. In addition to potential crime victims, the NFL players themselves, players' teams, and their teammates are all hurt when players commit crimes. The NFL and the NFL Players Association (NFLPA) must develop and upgrade existing programs and policies directed at modifying player behaviors that result in arrests.

The publicity given to athletes, including NFL players, who commit crimes is often quite extensive. A May 6, 2015, Google search I did for the player knocking his fiancé unconscious in an Atlantic City casino elevator yielded more than one hundred million results. This is more than four/fold the 23.9 million Google results I obtained when searching for "the NFL's most valuable player during the 2014 season." Even the name of the player accused of hitting his four-year-old son with a switch, and who played in only one regular season game in 2014, generated more Google results (28.4 million) than the league's most valuable player.

There is also extensive coverage of the NFL players who have been arrested in other media, like TV, sports and talk radio, and social media. This degree of overwhelming media coverage may give the impression that such arrests are pervasive and out of control. In a recent *Wall Street Journal* essay, one author proclaimed, "The NFL seems to be a thug-filled freak show denounced by everyone everywhere" (Cohen 2015). Scientific research, however, sometimes reveals lower arrest rates among NFL players versus the general population. The media play a big role in promulgating misconceptions about the scope of player problems, including arrests and arrest rates. As one Internet author notes, "Frequent media coverage of NFL players in legal trouble has created an unjustified stigma for the league and its players" (Riddle 2013). There is clearly a problem in the NFL with arrests. Moreover, many NFL players serve as role models for fans, and their actions could influence others. It remains uncertain, however, whether NFL arrests reflect an epidemic or out-of-control problem of any kind.

It is worth restating that arrests are not convictions, and all arrestees are presumed innocent until proven guilty. This chapter tells us nothing about the outcomes of the arrests that were studied with respect to convictions or jail time. There is some scientific evidence, however, indicating that there may be bias with respect to conviction rates and how they apply to athlete arrestees. Benedict and Klein (1997) studied 217 college and professional athletes who were charged with sexual assault and compared their conviction rates to individuals in the US general population also charged with sexual assault. They found the conviction rate for the athletes to be only 31 percent, compared to 51 percent for the general population.

In this study, I found age to be a significant risk factor for arrests for nonviolent crimes. In fact, these arrest rates drop by half among players aged twenty-eight years and older compared to those aged twenty-four years and younger. The results for violent crimes are different because the age group in the middle (twenty-five to twenty-seven years) has higher arrest rates than the youngest and oldest age groups. According to one author, "The relationship between aging and criminal activity has been noted since the beginning of criminology" (Ulmer and Steffensmeiser 2014, 377). In general, crime in the general population tends to rise during the late teens and peaks around twenty years of age. After that, it declines slowly but consistently with each age increase (Ulmer and Steffensmeiser 2014). In some ways, and notwithstanding temporal trends among NFL players documented in this chapter, the nature of the arrest results for NFL players, particularly for nonviolent crimes, is similar to those previously described for the general population.

Sports Illustrated (SI) published a piece (Law 2014) that highlights some of the issues that may arise in analysis of arrests conducted by lay individuals from a public-health perspective. The second paragraph of the article, titled "Arrests by Position," provides the number of arrests in the NFL since the year 2000, making use of the *USA Today* arrests database. The graph shows that wide receivers have the highest number of arrests (n = 122) of any NFL position (Law 2014) See table 2-5 of this chapter. Unlike the *SI* article, the data presented in this chapter deal only with a five-year period, from 2010 to 2014, and capture only arrests for regular-season players. Nevertheless, table 2-5 also indicates that wide receivers were arrested thirty-nine times, which is more than any other position, with the exception of linebackers, who had forty-three. The data presented in table 2-5 indicate that while wide receivers have a relatively high *number* of arrests, their *rate* of arrest for violent crimes is lower (31 per 1,000 players per year) than that of fullbacks (39.2 per 1,000 players per year), defensive tackles (37.6 per 1,000 players per year), and halfbacks (35.5 per 1,000 players per year). Furthermore, in this study, wide receivers' overall arrest rate for violent crimes (5.6 per 1,000 players per year) is lower than the league average (6.3 per 1,000 players per year) and is also lower than ten of the sixteen specific player positions. The fact that *SI* did not break down its data by violent and nonviolent crimes is perfectly reasonable. Moreover, the numerator data the magazine presents are almost certainly correct. However, the magazine staff members' inability to incorporate meaningful denominators into their calculations leads to conclusions that may be misleading.

The differences among NFL teams in the number and rate of arrests require additional research. Each team has its own culture that could influence play on the field, as well as arrests off of the field. At least one of the NFL sports websites has published an article titled the "Ten Dirtiest Teams of All Time" (Howard 2015). Interestingly, NFL teams that wear black uniforms have been found to be among the most penalized teams during a sixteen-year study period (Frank and Gilovich 1988). No research exists on the relationship between team culture and arrest rates. The Houston Texans had no arrests during the five-year study period covered in this chapter. Perhaps it's a coincidence that the Texans also had the lowest concussion rates of any NFL team during the period from 2010 to 2012 (Markowitz and Markowitz 2013). The owner of the Texans publicly called for "zero tolerance" with respect to domestic violence in the wake of several high-exposure incidents (Belvedere and David 2014).

Race could be an important variable to analyze for a chapter like this. According to a *USA Today* Internet article written in 2013, black NFL players get arrested ten times more often than white players. The authors further note, "Sociologists attribute [the disproportionate arrest rate] to several social factors in the black population at large, including a disproportionate rate of poverty and single-parent backgrounds." (Schrotenboer 2013).

However, race data were not available to me for the players covered in this chapter. Consequently, I was unable to examine the relationship between race and arrests.

In this study, position is definitely an important variable in terms of arrest rates. Defensive linemen, offensive backs, and defensive backs have ten, nine, and eighteen times more arrests for violent crimes, respectively, when compared to offensive linemen. It seems unlikely that position would directly impact arrest rates. Instead, a third variable, perhaps race, could be helping to account for differences in arrest rates related to position. According to unofficial statistics provided by the BestTicketsBlog (Powell-Morse 2014), the large majority of individuals who play defensive line, offensive back, and defensive back positions are African American.

The finding that arrests do not occur uniformly throughout the year is both interesting and important. Seasonal victimization trends have been documented in the general-population criminology literature (Lauritsen 2014). For example, victimization rates for household crimes like larceny and burglary tended to be higher during summer months compared to other times of the year. This same pattern exists for aggravated-assault rates (Lauritsen 2014). In this study, the relatively small numbers of arrests among NFL players makes it difficult to conduct meaningful analyses of specific crimes and seasonality.

The results presented in this chapter, however, do indicate higher rates of arrests during off-season months, especially months immediately preceding and following football-playing months. In the case of arrests for nonviolent crimes, these results reach levels of statistical significance. The number of arrests for violent crimes had a similar pattern but failed to reach significance, probably owing to the relatively small number of these arrests. One Internet sports reporter commented on the increase in arrests during the period just before the beginning of training camp, saying, "NFL coaches and team officials have a love–hate relationship with this time of year, the five- or six-week stretch that links the end of mandatory minicamp with the start of training camp" (Zrebiec 2013). This same article notes the difficulties inherent in the period when NFL rosters are at the maximum levels and players are dispersed throughout the country: "There are no daily meetings or practices to occupy a player's time, attention, and energy. What there is a lot of for players is free time, distractions, and different influences pulling on them" (Zrebiec 2013).

In the general population, significant life changes have been linked to an increasing severity of offenses, as well as a rise in lethal violence (National Institute of Justice 2014b). The changes between football-playing months and the off-season, as they relate to players' routines and workloads, intertwined with social support and team supervision, could contribute to changes in behavior and possibly even participation in criminal activities.

CONCLUDING REMARKS

Arrests are common in the United States, and NFL players are not exempt from this unfortunate reality. While the number of violent crimes has steadily declined in the country as a whole in recent years, the same cannot be said for NFL players. In fact, arrest rates for violent crimes among NFL players have risen each year between 2010 and 2014, with the exception of 2012. In all, violent-crime rates in the NFL rose nearly 27 percent between 2010 and 2014. Rates of nonviolent-crime arrests have been more stable during the study period, although the rates observed during the two most recent years studied, 2013 and 2014, have been the highest of the five years examined in this chapter. Given the national trends on arrests in the general population, the rise in arrests rates among NFL players is worrisome.

With jail sentences lengthening in this country, players who are convicted and incarcerated could now spend more time behind bars than arrestees did in previous years. Assaults and domestic violence are the two most common types of violent crimes associated with arrests among NFL players, and DUI and drugs dominate the nonviolent arrests. Violent or not, these offenses are quite serious and could have life-or-death implications for affected players and victims. The variables associated with being arrested, like player position, off-season months, and team may provide clues regarding which players are at risk of being arrested and how best to address this problem. Given the temporal trends in arrest rates among NFL players, existing programs and policies may not be effective, and ongoing monitoring and upgrading of these activities need to be considered.

REFERENCES

Amendla, D. 2013. "Brian Baldinger: Player Arrests Are Out of Control." DA Show, Damon Amendola, July 2. http://da.radio.cbssports.com/2013/07/02/brian-baldinger-player-arrests-are-out-of-control/.

Belvedere, M. J., and J. E. David. 2014. "NFL's Culture Is Broken, Needs 'Zero Tolerance' Policy: Texans Owner." CNBC, September 17. http://www.cnbc.com/id/102007868.

Benedict, J., and A. Klein. 1997. "Arrest and Conviction Rates for Athletes Accused of Sexual Assault." *Sociology of Sport Journal* 14 (1): 86–93.

BlackDemographics.com. http://blackdemographics.com/.

Brame, R., S. D. Bushway, R. Paternoster, and M. G. Turner. 2014. "Demographic Patterns of Cumulative Arrest Prevalence by Ages 18 and 23." *Crime and Delinquency*: 471–86.

Bureau of Justice Statistics. 2010. "Prison Inmates at Midyear 2009—Statistical Tables." http://www.bjs.gov/index.cfm?ty=pbdetail&iid=2200.

———. 2011. "Correctional Populations in the United States, 2010." http://www.bjs.gov/index.cfm?ty=pbdetail&iid=2237.

Cohen, R. 2015. "How the NFL Reflects American Culture." *Wall Street Journal*, May 7.

FBI Uniform Crime Reports. 2010. "Crime in the United States." http://www.fbi.gov/about-us/cjis/ucr/crime-in-the-u.s/2010/crime-in-the-u.s.-2010/tables/10tbl39.xls.

———. 2011. "Crime in the United States" http://www.fbi.gov/about-us/cjis/ucr/crime-in-the-u.s/2011/crime-in-the-u.s.-2011/tables/table-39.

———. 2012. "Crime in the United States." http://www.fbi.gov/about-us/cjis/ucr/crime-in-the-u.s/2012/crime-in-the-u.s.-2012/tables/39tabledatadecoverviewpdf.

———. 2013. "Crime in the United States." http://www.fbi.gov/about-us/cjis/ucr/crime-in-the-u.s/2013/crime-in-the-u.s.-2013/tables/table-39.

Frank, M. G., and T. Gilovich. 1988. "The Dark Side of Self- and Social Perception: Black Uniforms and Aggression in Professional Sports." *Journal of Personality and Social Psychology* 54 (1): 74–85.

Heavy Sports. 2014. "NFL Census: Data on Players' Race, Weight & Height." http://heavy.com/sports/2014/09/what-percentage-of-nfl-players-are-black-white/.

Howard, M. 2015. "The Dirtiest Football Teams of All Time." *Daily Beast*, January 28. http://www.thedailybeast.com/articles/2015/01/28/the-dirtiest-football-teams-of-all-time.html.

Lauritsen, J. L. 2014. "Seasonal Patterns in Criminal Victimization Trends." Bureau of Justice Statistics, June 17. http://www.bjs.gov/index.cfm?ty=pbdetail&iid=5028.

Laws, W. 2014. "Is the New NFL Conduct Policy Enough to Exact Real Change?" SI, October 1. http://www.si.com/nfl/2014/10/01/nfl-arrest-data-roger-goodell-ray-rice-adrian-peterson.

Markowitz, J. S., and A. Markowitz. 2013. *Pigskin Crossroads: The Epidemiology of Concussions in the National Football League (NFL), 2010–12*. CreateSpace.

National Institute of Justice. 2014a. "From Juvenile Delinquency to Young Adult Offending." http://www.nij.gov/topics/crime/Pages/delinquency to adult-offending.aspx.

National Institute of Justice. 2014b. "Office of Justice Programs." http://www.nij.gov/topics/crime/violent/Pages/welcome.aspx.

National Research Council. *The Growth of Incarceration in the United States: Exploring Causes and Consequences*. Washington, DC: National Academies Press, 2014.

NFL. 2014. "NFL Owners Endorse New Personal Conduct Policy." December 10. http://www.nfl.com/news/story/0ap3000000441758/article/nfl-owners-endorse-new-personal-conduct-policy.

The Pew Charitable Trusts. 2012. "Time Served: The High Cost, Low Return of Longer Prison Terms." http://www.pewtrusts.org/en/

research-and-analysis/reports/2012/06/06/time-served-the-high-cost-low-return-of-longer-prison-terms.

Powell-Morse, A. "The Unofficial 2014 NFL Player Census, September 23, 2014." BestTicketsBlog, Data Visualizations. http://www.besttickets.com/blog/nfl-player-census-2014/.

Riddle, R. 2013. "The Facts and Fictions Surrounding a Culture of Violence in the NFL." Bleacher Report, June 28. http://bleacherreport.com/articles/1687580-the-facts-and-fictions-surrounding-a-culture-of-violence-in-the-nfl.

San Diego Union-Tribune. 2010-14. "NFL Arrests Database." http://www.sandiegouniontribune.com/nfl/arrests-database/.

Schotenboer, B. 2013. "Black NFL Players Arrested Nearly 10 Times Often as Whites." *USA Today*, November 19. http://www.usatoday.com/story/sports/nfl/2013/11/29/racial-profiling-nfl/3779489/.

Sentencing Project. n. d. "The Federal Prison Population: A Statistical Analysis." http://www.sentencingproject.org/doc/publications/inc_federalprisonpop.pdf.

Ulmer, J. T., and D. Steffensmeir. "The Age and Crime Relationship: Social Variation, Social Explanations." In *The Nurture versus Biosocial Debate in Criminology: On the Origins of Criminal Behavior and Criminality*, edited by K. Beaver, J. Barnes, and B. Boutwell, 377–97. London: SAGE.

USA Today. 2010-14. "NFL Player Arrests." http://www.usatoday.com/sports/nfl/arrests/.

Wikipedia. 2015a. "Black Players in American Professional Football." http://en.wikipedia.org/wiki/Black_players_in_American_professional_football.

Wikipedia. 2015b. "Demographics of the United States." http://en.wikipedia.org/wiki/Demographics_of_the_United_States.

Zrebiec, J. 2013. "Latest Arrests Highlight Difficult Time of Year for NFL Coaches and Executives." *Baltimore Sun*, June 27. http://articles.baltimoresun.com/2013-06-27/sports/bal-arrests-highlight-tense-time-for-nfl-coaches-and-executives-20130626_1_bernard-pierce-john-harbaugh-mandatory-minicamp.

Table 2-1. Frequency Distributions of Arrests for Violent and Nonviolent Crimes among Eligible NFL Players, 2010–14

All Arrests for Violent Crimes			All Arrests for Nonviolent Crimes		
Arrest Type	N	%	Arrest Type	N	%
Assault	19	31.2%	Alcohol	2	1.1%
Assault / Alcohol	1	1.6%	Child support	1	0.6%
Assault / Gun	3	4.9%	Criminal mischief	1	0.6%
Battery	4	6.6%	DUI	63	35.0%
Burglary / Gun	1	1.6%	DUI / Drugs	3	1.7%
Child abuse	2	3.3%	Disorderly conduct	9	5.0%
DUI / Assault	1	1.6%	Disturbing the peace	1	0.6%
Domestic violence	23	37.7%	Drugs	30	16.7%
Gun (Violent)	1	1.6%	Drugs / Gun	2	1.1%
Gun / Privacy invasion	1	1.6%	Failure to appear	3	1.7%
Murder / Gun	2	3.3%	False name	1	0.6%
Reckless driving / Weapon use	1	1.6%	Fraud	1	0.6%
Sexual assault	2	3.3%	Gun (Nonviolent)	11	6.1%
Total	61	100%	License	10	5.6%
			Obstruction	2	1.1%
			Outstanding warrant	5	2.8%
			Public intoxication	10	5.6%
			Reckless driving	3	1.7%
			Reckless endangerment	1	0.6%
			Resisting arrest	4	2.2%
			Sex	2	1.1%
			Solicitation	1	0.6%
			Speeding	1	0.6%
			Stalking	1	0.6%
			Theft	5	2.8%
			Trespassing	3	1.7%
			Urinating in public	1	0.6%
			Weapon	1	0.6%
			Other	2	1.1%
			Total	180	100%

Table 2-2. Number of Violent and Nonviolent Crime Arrests and Arrest Rates, 2010–14						
Season	2010	2011	2012	2013	2014	2010-14*
Total Number of Players	1,926	1,910	1,938	1,911	1,936	9,621
Number of Arrests						
Nonviolent crimes	33	34	34	44	35	180
Violent crimes	11	12	11	13	14	61
Arrest Rates per 1,000 Players						
Nonviolent crimes	17.1	17.8	17.5	23.0	18.1	18.7
Violent crimes	5.7	6.3	5.7	6.8	7.2	6.3
* annualized rate						

Table 2-3. Statistical Summary of Arrest Rates in the NFL for Violent and Nonviolent Crimes among Regular-Season Players, 2010–14

	Arrest Rates per 1,000 Players		Statistical Results			
	Nonviolent Crimes	Violent Crimes	Nonviolent Crimes		Violent Crimes	
All	18.7	6.3	N/A			
Year			Incidence Rate Ratio	95% CI	Incidence Rate Ratio	95% CI
2010	17.1	5.7	Index Reference		Index Reference	
2011	17.8	6.3	1.0	0.6, 1.7	1.1	0.4, 2.8
2012	17.5	5.7	1.0	0.6, 1.7	1.0	0.4, 2.6
2013	23.0	6.8	1.3	0.8, 2.2	1.2	0.5, 2.9
2014	18.1	7.2	1.1	0.6, 1.8	1.3	0.5, 3.1
Age (in years)						
< 25	24.1	5.3	Index Reference		Index Reference	
25 to 27	18.7	8.2	0.8	0.6, 1.1	1.6	0.8, 3.0
28 +	12.1	5.5	0.5	0.3, 0.8	1.0	0.5, 2.1
Weight (in pounds)						
< 216	20.5	7.4	Index Reference		Index Reference	
216 to 259	19.0	6.3	0.9	0.6, 1.3	0.9	0.4, 1.6
260 +	16.7	5.3	0.8	0.6, 1.2	0.7	0.4, 1.4
Six-Group Position						
Offensive linemen	7.4	0.6	Index Reference		Index Reference	
Defensive linemen	24.4	6.8	3.31	1.7, 7.0	11.0	1.6, 479
Offensive backs	25.2	5.7	3.4	1.7, 7.3	9.2	1.2, 417
Defensive backs	17.0	11.1	2.3	1.2, 4.7	18.1	3.0, 733
Receivers	26.1	4.1	3.5	1.8, 7.3	6.7	0.9, 304
Kickers	5.4	0.0	0.7	0.1, 3.3	0	0, 172
Time of Year						
Football season	14.1	5.0				
Off-season	23.3	7.7	1.6	1.2, 2.3	1.50	0.9, 2.7

Team	N Players	N Arrests for Nonviolent Crimes	N Arrests for Violent Crimes	Arrest Rate for Nonviolent Crimes*	Arrest Rates for Violent Crimes*
49ers	287	8	2	27.9	7.0
Bears	307	7	2	22.8	6.5
Bengals	295	6	6	20.3	20.3
Bills	304	5	0	16.4	0
Broncos	282	10	5	35.5	17.7
Browns	298	8	2	26.8	6.7
Bucs	316	12	1	38.0	3.2
Cardinals	294	3	3	10.2	10.2
Chargers	314	3	1	9.6	3.2
Chiefs	290	4	1	13.8	3.4
Colts	327	9	0	27.5	0
Cowboys	308	6	1	19.5	3.2
Dolphins	309	3	5	9.7	16.2
Eagles	291	4	2	13.7	6.9
Falcons	275	5	1	18.2	3.6
Giants	308	3	0	9.7	0
Jaguars	323	5	0	15.5	0
Jets	302	4	3	13.2	9.9
Lions	303	7	2	23.1	6.6
Packers	289	3	3	10.4	10.4
Panthers	312	1	1	3.2	3.2
Patriots	311	1	3	3.2	9.6
Raiders	302	6	2	19.9	6.6
Rams	295	4	1	13.6	3.4
Ravens	293	5	2	17.1	6.8
Redskins	309	10	1	32.4	3.2
Saints	294	1	1	3.4	3.4
Seahawks	312	9	2	28.8	6.4
Steelers	287	4	1	13.9	3.5
Texans	302	0	0	0	0
Titans	305	10	1	32.8	3.3
Vikings	277	11	5	39.7	18.1
Free agents	--	3	1	n/a	n/a
Totals	9,621	180	61	18.7	6.3

Table 2-4. Number of Arrests and Arrest Rates for Violent and Nonviolent Crimes by NFL Teams, 2010–14

* per 1,000 players

		Table 2-5. NFL Arrest Rates for Violent and Nonviolent Crimes By Position, 2010–14			
Six-Group Position Type	Specific Positions	N Arrests for Nonviolent Crimes	N Arrests for Violent Crimes	Arrest Rate for Nonviolent Crimes*	Arrest Rates for Violent Crimes*
Defensive linemen	Defensive tackles	19	4	37.5	7.9
	Defensive ends	17	6	19.5	6.9
	Nose tackles	0	0	0	0
Defensive backs	Linebackers	25	18	18.2	13.1
	Cornerbacks	20	10	25.6	12.8
	Safeties	9	7	15.4	12.0
Offensive backs	Running backs	25	6	35.5	8.5
	Quarterbacks	0	1	0	2.7
	Fullbacks	6	0	39.2	0
Receivers	Wide receivers	33	6	31.0	5.6
	Tight ends	11	1	17.7	1.6
Offensive linemen	Guards	2	1	3.3	1.6
	Tackles	9	0	14.7	0
	Centers	1	0	4.3	0
Kickers	Punters	1	0	5.6	0
	Place kickers	1	0	5.3	0

* per 1,000 players

CHAPTER 3

Domestic-Violence Arrests: A Fifteen-Year Study

• • •

ACCORDING TO THE WORLD HEALTH Organization (2013), the problem of domestic violence has reached epoch proportions in the United States and around the world. The thousands of people victimized and affected by domestic violence often suffer far-reaching consequences that tear at the fabric of their lives, families, and communities. By no means is domestic violence a problem restricted to professional athletes and celebrities, although the seemingly constant stream of such sports-related reports in the media sometimes makes it seem that way. In many instances, domestic violence can result in pain, injury, permanent disability, and even death (World Health Organization 2013).

In 2014, the *Huffington Post* published a piece titled "Is Domestic Violence a Bigger Problem than We Realize? Illustrates How Deep the Problem Goes." This article provides a well-documented set of facts and statistics highlighting some of the impacts of domestic violence in the United States: Nearly one out of every three female homicide victims are killed by their intimate partners. One-fourth of all women experience sexual violence at the hands of their partners during their lifetimes. More than three million US children witness domestic violence within their homes each year. And many of the children living in homes where domestic violence occurs suffer a wide range of adverse social, psychological, and health consequences (Hall 2014).

In a landmark survey conducted by the Centers for Disease Control in 2003, it was estimated that intimate-partner violence results in roughly 5.3 million victimizations of women over the age of eighteen each year. These incidents lead to about two million injuries, more than one-fourth of which require medical attention. Domestic violence causes more injury than car accidents, muggings, and rapes combined. In fact, it is the leading cause of injury among women. On a national basis, roughly 85 percent of domestic-violence victims are women, and the highest-risk age group is between twenty and twenty-four years old (DoSomething. Org, 2015).

These statistics came from different sources, were collected over different periods of time, and used a variety of methodologies including surveys and arrest records. While it is difficult to estimate the exact scope and magnitude of the domestic violence problem, it is safe to say that it represents a serious and widespread malady that affects millions of people, especially women, on a worldwide basis. Indirect damages and costs associated with domestic violence are also quite extensive and far-reaching.

Scientific literature on rates of domestic violence among NFL players is actually quite limited. Lay sports and Internet writers have attempted to shed some light on the scope of this problem. While this work may increase the attention focused on domestic violence as an important national problem, the existing literature can be confusing and may not offer many real answers. In this chapter, I attempt to add to existing knowledge on the scope of domestic-violence arrests among NFL players. I accomplished this by computing arrest rates for a fifteen-year period and identifying potential risk factors. I examined the relationships among team, position, and birthplace in relation to the incidence of domestic violence.

METHODS

For this study, I used the *USA Today* "NFL Player Arrests" database (*USA Today* 2000-14) for NFL players. This database contains arrest information on NFL players beginning in the year 2000. It provides a

"Category" column that describes the arrest type and a "Description" column that briefly details the nature of the arrests. I used both the "Category" and "Description" columns to identify domestic-violence arrests. I considered all domestic-violence arrests between January 1, 2000, and December 31, 2014, listed in the *USA Today* database for inclusion in this study.

I calculated domestic-violence arrest rates for regular-season NFL players for each of the fifteen study years (2000–14). I also computed annualized five-year arrest rates (for 2000–04, 2005–09, and 2010–14). Finally, I calculated a fifteen-year total domestic-violence annualized arrest rate. The numerators I used are the numbers of domestic-violence arrests of eligible NFL players between 2000 and 2014.

I aggregated month-of-arrest data into two groups: off-season (February through July) and football-playing season (August through January). I conducted risk-factor analyses on three variables (calendar year, age at time of arrest, and position). I provided incidence-rate ratios (IRRs) with 95 percent confidence intervals (95 percent CIs). I divided the states in which players were born into four regions (the Midwest, the Northeast, the South, and the West) based on standard groupings used by the US Census (US Census Bureau 2015). I provided frequency distributions (not arrest rates) for the number of arrests by region based on the five-year periods, as well as all fifteen study years combined. Because denominators for some potential risk-factor variables used in this study are not available between 2000 and 2009, I provided numerator data only for these variables.

RESULTS

A total of ninety-one arrests among NFL players appear in the *USA Today* "NFL Player Arrests" database for domestic violence between 2000 and 2014. I dropped six of these arrests from the analyses, which leaves eighty-five domestic-violence arrests. These six arrests include two domestic-violence arrestees who did not play in at least one regular season between 2000 and 2014, one player arrested in 2013 who had not played in the NFL since 2011, and three players arrested after the study cutoff date of December 31, 2014. These exclusions are reasonable for this study and help facilitate denominator calculations. A number of NFL players with domestic-violence arrests did not play in the league the year immediately following their arrests ($n = 8$). This was mainly due to disciplinary actions taken by the NFL, not making an NFL team roster, or legal actions taken against them. Such players are included in the analyses.

Table 3-1 shows the number of arrests and arrest rates for domestic violence for each year between 2000 and 2014. Domestic-violence arrest rates range from a low of 1.0 per 1,000 players in 2004 to a high of 5.2 per 1,000 players in three different years (2005, 2006, and 2008). The earliest five-year study period (2000–04) and the most recent five year period (2010–14), have similar annualized domestic-violence arrest rates of 2.5 and 2.4 per 1,000 players, respectively. The middle five-year period (2005–09) has the highest annualized domestic-violence rate—4.1 per 1,000 players. For the entire fifteen-year study period, the arrest rate for domestic violence in the NFL averages 3.0 per 1,000 players per year. With a total of eighty-five domestic-violence arrests during the fifteen-year study period, the average number of arrests per year among regular season players is 5.7.

The eighty-five domestic-violence arrests that occurred during the fifteen-year study period involved seventy-seven NFL players. Seventy players were arrested once, six were arrested twice, and one player was arrested three times. This means that about 9 percent of the players arrested for domestic violence were arrested more than once.

Because the domestic-violence arrest rates are similar for the five-year periods 2000–04 and 2010–14, the incidence-rate ratio was close to 1.0 (0.96) and was not significant. The domestic-violence arrest rates for the middle five-year period, 2005–09, was more than 60 percent higher than the rate for the earlier five-year period, 2000–2004, but just fails to be significantly different.

Table 3-2 shows the number of domestic-violence arrests by month for the five-year study periods. There tends to be more arrests for domestic violence during the off-season months of February to July (n = fifty-two out of eighty-five arrests, or 61.2 percent) for all fifteen study years combined, compared to thirty-three arrests (38.8 percent) for domestic violence occurring during the football playing months, August through January.

Table 3-3 shows the domestic violence risk-factor results by arrest age. These analyses are conducted for the 2010 to 2014 combined period only. The group of players in the age group twenty-five to twenty-seven years has the highest domestic-violence arrest rates, averaging 3.2 per 1,000 players per year. The youngest age group (twenty-four years and younger) averaged 2.2 domestic-violence arrests and the oldest group (twenty years and older) have the lowest rates (1.7 arrests per 1,000 players per year). However, age was not a significant risk factor for rates of domestic-violence arrests.

Table 3-3 also shows the risk-factor results for player position. Defensive backs and defensive linemen have the highest arrests rates for domestic violence, averaging 3.7 and 3.4 arrests per 1,000 players per year, respectively. The next two highest positions are offensive backs and receivers, with domestic-violence arrest rates of 2.4 and 1.8, respectively. Offensive linemen and kickers do not have any arrests for domestic violence during the fifteen-year study period. None of the incidence-rate ratio results for the six-group position variable reached statistical significance.

Table 3-4 shows the number of domestic-violence arrests for the thirty-two NFL teams for each of the five-year study periods and all fifteen years combined. These results are sorted from the highest to lowest number of arrests. Arrest rates are not given for teams. There is considerable variation among teams in the number of domestic-violence arrests. The Broncos have the most arrests for domestic violence of any NFL team, with eleven for the fifteen-year study period. The next-closest team is the Dolphins with seven domestic-violence arrests, followed by the Cardinals, Seahawks, and Steelers with five arrests each. The Bills, Eagles, and Jaguars did not have any domestic-violence arrests during the entire fifteen-year study period.

Table 3-5 contains frequencies of domestic-violence arrests broken down by the region of the country where players were born. (I dropped from this analysis the one arrestee who was born outside of the United States.) The frequency distribution of these numerators reveals that when all fifteen study years are combined, about two-thirds of players with domestic-violence arrests were born in the Southern region of the country. In all, fifty-six of the eighty-four domestic-violence arrests (66.7 percent) involve players born in the South. The birthplace regions with the next-highest number of domestic-violence arrests are the Midwest and West, with twelve and eleven arrests, respectively. The Northeast has the fewest arrests for domestic violence ($n = 5$).

Discussion

In this chapter, I computed the rate of domestic-violence arrests among NFL players for a fifteen-year study period, 2000–14. I found that the rates are similar during the five-year periods 2000–04 and 2010–14, averaging 2.4 and 2.5 per 1,000 players on an annualized basis, respectively. Arrest rates during the period 2005–09 are substantially higher, averaging just over four arrests per 1,000 players per year.

Arrest rates for specific crimes can vary over time due to changes in policies and laws. For example, between the mid-1980s and the late-1990s, police inaction in response to domestic violence resulted in increased liabilities for individual states (Iyengar 2007). In the ensuing years, numerous states passed laws that required warrantless arrests of individuals suspected of committing assault of an intimate partner, using a "probable cause" standard. By 2010, there were twenty-one states with mandatory arrests for domestic-violence assaults (American Bar Association 2014). In 2008, David Hirschel wrote. "Police are making more arrests in domestic-violence incidents. When they cannot determine which person in an incident is at fault...they sometimes arrest them both" (Hirschel 2008). It cannot be ruled out that the spike in domestic-violence arrest rates among NFL players during the period 2005–09 may be related to these changing arrest policies. Currently, depending on the state, domestic-violence arrests may be mandatory, preferred, or at the officer's discretion (Hirschel 2008).

Overall, violent crimes in the United States have declined over time, recently returning to similar levels as reported in the late-1970s (Simpson, 2014). More specifically, the number of victimizations for "serious domestic violence" and "serious intimate-partner violence" dropped substantially between 2000 and 2010 and then again between 2010 and 2011 (US Department of Justice, Bureau of Justice Statistics 2012). It is estimated that over the past twenty years, domestic violence in the United States has declined by about 64 percent (US Bureau of Justice 2012). Even with the drop among NFL players in domestic-violence arrest rates between 2005 and 2009 and between 2010 and 2014 (from 4.1 to 2.4 per 1,000 players per year), the most recent arrest rates are similar to the ones obtained for the five-year period 2000–04. That is, there has been no decline in domestic-violence arrest rates among NFL players from those in 2000–04 to those in 2010–14. This disturbing pattern contrasts with national trends and begs for changes in existing NFL policies related to domestic violence.

It is beyond the scope of this chapter to attempt to compare domestic-violence arrest rates among NFL players with those of the larger US general population. In chapter 4, this comparison is made for driving under the influence (DUI) arrests, which has its own separate category and statistics published in the FBI's Uniform Crime Reporting (UCR) program. An arrest for domestic violence could be reported by the FBI under any of a number of crimes such as murder, manslaughter, rape, and several types of assaults. Also, domestic-violence statistics are often quantified in terms of number of victims and victimization rates (US Department of Justice, Bureau of Justice Statistics, 2012). Hence, comparisons between the domestic-violence arrests between NFL players and the general population can be a difficult undertaking.

When examining a relatively rare event, like arrests for domestic vio-lence in the NFL, it becomes critical to carefully determine who will and who will not be counted as a "case." Counting individuals in a domestic-violence arrest numerator who have never participated in a single play in a regular season NFL game has important implications for the denomina-tor to be used. The same can be said for players who may get arrested years following their last appearance in the NFL. Players like these are some-times included in the *USA Today* "NFL Player Arrests" database. In turn, this could lead to unsuspecting writers counting such players as domestic-violence cases when their affiliation with the NFL is marginal at best.

Virtually all epidemiological studies involving counts or rates of a given disease or event have specific inclusion and exclusion criteria stipu-lating who will be counted as a case (i.e., the numerator) and from which population they will be drawn (i.e., the denominator). Few, if any, of the sports, and Internet reports that have attempted to assess the scope of the domestic-violence problem in the NFL, have incorporated such criteria into their work. Consequently, their numerator counts of domestic vio-lence and other arrests can be subject to error, which, in turn, can result in incorrect rates and misleading conclusions. Clearly, the commission of even one domestic-violence incident is too many among NFL players, and there can be little doubt that there is a problem here that requires imme-diate attention. The need for data that attempt to calculate the scope of a problem like domestic violence in the NFL is critical. Lay computations of these statistics are not the answer.

One ambitious article that appeared on a popular sports site/blog, *FiveThirtyEightSports*, attempted to go further than count domestic-violence cases among NFL players (Morris 2014). This article used the *USA Today* "NFL Player Arrests" database, along with an Arrest Data Analysis tool that is available through the US Bureau of Justice Statistics. For its analyses of relative arrest rates among NFL players versus the US general population for specific crimes, including domestic violence, *FiveThirtyEightSports* used 2,560 total players as the denominator for the thirty-two NFL teams. This was derived by multiplying the thirty-two teams by eighty. According to the authors, this is the number of players in training camp "at the league's peak" (Morris 2014). However, "According to NFL rules, each team can...have ninety players when training camp starts" (Davis II 2014). The NFL implemented a rule change modifying the maximum number of training-camp players from eighty to ninety in 2012. The change is documented in an article that appeared on the NFL website in April of that year (Sessler 2012). This means that the denominator used by *FiveThirtyEight* (Morris 2014) will underestimate the number of players by 320 (i.e., ten players for each of the thirty-two NFL teams) for both 2012 and 2013, for a total underestimate of 640 players. This represents an 11.1 percent underestimate of the actual denominator for these two years, and of course, a comparable overestimate of the arrest rate.

Another major issue with this same *FiveThirtyEightSports* article has to do with the general population used to compare NFL players (Morris 2014). Only statistics for males in the twenty-five- to twenty-nine-year age group are used for the general-population calculations. The justification for this that the article provides is as follows: "This group is the most similar to the NFL as a whole, where the average team age varies from twenty-five to twenty-seven years old" (Morris 2014). However, data collected in this study indicate that at least half of all the regular-season NFL players between 2010 and 2014 fall outside the age range of twenty-five to twenty-nine years. In fact, more than 37 percent of all NFL players are in the age range of twenty-four years and younger. Excluding individuals from this younger age range in the general-population estimates of domestic-violence arrests will have an impact on the rates that are calculated. This is because more violent crimes are committed by males in the twenty- to twenty-four-year age range. For example, in 2010, the FBI reported nearly sixty-nine thousand arrests for violent crimes among males in the twenty- to twenty-four-year age group, compared to just over fifty-two thousand in twenty- to twenty-nine-year-old males (FBI 2010). The omission of males over the age of twenty-nine in *FiveThirtyEightSports*' general-population domestic-violence arrest estimates has the opposite effect because violent-crime arrest rates tend to decline with age. The result of using only the twenty-five- to twenty-nine-year age group to derive general-population estimates of domestic-violence arrests becomes subject to both over- and underestimation.

Another unfortunate aspect of papers like this is that they repeatedly get cited by others, including, in this case, the *New Republic* (Vinik 2014), the National Organization for Women (2014), the *International Business Times* (Barrabi 2014), an NBC affiliate (Brock and Kiriakos 2014), and others. Hence, misinformation gets proliferated by the media in an almost-uncontrollable manner. For a problem as serious as domestic violence, the highest-quality data and reporting are indicated and required, not the lowest.

The way the NFL has handled a number of high-profile domestic violence cases has been subject to intense criticism by a variety of groups. The initial two-game suspension involving the NFL player caught on video camera knocking out his fiancé in a casino elevator resulted in many calls for Commissioner Goodell's resignation. This included one by the veteran sports reporter Keith Olberman. He said, "If there had been some recognition today, some form of acknowledgment for the women fans of the NFL, that this two-game suspension is a virtual attack on them, perhaps these following words would not be necessary. But for the sake of the NFL, and more importantly for the sake of those women and all others, all of us in a country in which this is so much more than a mere sports league, it is necessary, Mr. Goodell, for you to now resign as its commissioner" (Olberman, quoted in *SB Nation* 2014).

Others demanding the resignation of Commissioner Goodell because of his handling of this incident included the National Organization for Woman and the feminist group UltraViolet (CBS New York 2014). In a statement, National Organization for Women (NOW) president Terry O'Neill said, "The NFL has lost its way. It doesn't have a [player's name] problem; it has a violence against women problem" (National Organization for Women 2014). In response to these and other pressures, the league changed the minimum suspension for domestic violence, assault, and sexual assault to six games and also added a lifetime ban for a second offense

(*Week* 2014). Moreover, the league subsequently suspended the player who knocked out his fiancé indefinitely. These new policies require ongoing monitoring and evaluation to ensure that they actually reduce the incidence of domestic-violence incidents committed by NFL players. The NFL could also take the lead on other educational and research programs targeted at reducing the occurrence of domestic violence among NFL players.

Statistical analyses of domestic-violence arrest rates by player position fail to yield significant results. Nevertheless, there is considerable variation in rates with respect to position. Defensive linemen and defensive backs both have domestic-violence arrest rates that are higher than the other position types and also exceed the league average. At the other end of the distribution, kickers and offensive linemen have no arrests for domestic violence during the entire fifteen-year study period. Again, player position is unlikely to have an impact on domestic-violence arrest rates in a direct manner, and some other third variable, like race, could be the primary factor.

The Broncos have eleven domestic-violence arrests during the fifteen-year study period. This is at least double the number of such arrests for each of the other thirty-one teams except the Dolphins, who have seven arrests. The eleven domestic-violence arrests among the Broncos involve eight different players. This is because three Broncos players have two domestic-violence arrests each. In the entire NFL, there are seven recidivist players with respect to domestic-violence arrests during the study period. This means that a single team, the Broncos, has nearly 43 percent of the players with repeat domestic-violence arrests. Tools, like the Danger Assessment Scale, are being developed to help identify offenders at risk of repeating their crimes (Goodman et al. 2000). This particular assessment is administered to battered victims and may help identify short-term abuse recidivism (Goodman et al. 2000). If and when tools like this become fully validated, the NFL could consider administering them to domestic-violence victims of NFL arrestees. The NFL could also get involved in research that develops and validates these kinds of assessments.

About 61 percent of all domestic-violence arrests involve players born in the Southern region of the United States, as defined by the US Bureau of the Census. As a comparison, unofficial NFL census data for 2014 (Powell-Morse 2014) indicate that about 51 percent of all NFL players were born in Southern states. Again, these are unofficial figures, and they are only for 2014. Nevertheless, these data do not allow us to rule out the possibility that players born in Southern states are overrepresented in NFL domestic-violence arrest rates.

There are data that suggest that domestic violence is "passed among family members and across generations" (Davis et al. 2005, 30). In general, predictors, correlates, and social indicators of domestic and family violence may include factors like divorce and changes in family structure, family instability, parental incarceration, single-parent homes, less time spent with children, poverty, violent families, low measures of academic achievement, family history of alcohol and violence, substance abuse, poor family relationships, stress, mental health problems, financial problems, and many other factors (Davis et al. 2005). It is beyond the scope of this chapter to determine how these and other factors may be related to the apparent overrepresentation of Southern players arrested for domestic violence. Additional research on this topic is definitely required.

Concluding Remarks

Regardless of the population studied and the quality of the data, domestic violence tends to be underreported. This is likely to be the case for NFL players as well.

Domestic violence is a heinous crime in which the fundamental human rights of the victims are grossly violated. While US statistics generally indicate a substantial decline in violent crimes, including domestic violence, over recent decades (US Justice Department in CBSNEWS 2013), advocacy groups (Advocates for Human Rights 2013) and other informed groups like the World Health Organization (2013) believe it is a "worldwide epidemic." Unlike general US population statistics, this chapter has documented no change in domestic-violence arrest rates among regular-season players in the NFL over the past fifteen years. In several recent high-profile cases, the league's policies related to the handling of players charged with domestic violence have met with considerable criticism from prominent sports writers, women's advocacy groups, and many others. In the aftermath of one of these incidents, the league publicly announced that mistakes were made and policy changes were later implemented. Commissioner Goodell stated, "The same mistakes can never be repeated" (Wilner 2014). It remains to be seen whether any of these changes will help reduce or eliminate altogether the number of domestic-violence incidents among NFL players.

REFERENCES

Advocates for Human Rights. 2013. "Prevalence of Domestic Violence." http://www.stopvaw.org/prevalence_of_domestic_violence.

American Bar Association Commission on Domestic Violence. 2014. "Domestic-Violence Arrest Policies by State." http://www.americanbar. org/content/dam/aba/administrative/domestic_violence1/Resources/ statutorysummarycharts/2014% 20Domestic%20Violence%20Arrest% 20Policy%20Chart.authcheckdam.pdf.

Barrabi, T. 2014. "NFL Domestic-Violence Timeline: A Look at Major Incidents and Arrests Since 1994." *International Business Times*, September 17. http://www.ibtimes.com/nfl-domestic-violence-time line-look-major-incidents-arrests-1994-1690807.

Brock, S., and K. Kiriakos. 2014. "Reality Check: NFL Player Arrests on Rise?" NBC Bay Area, September 22. http://www.nbcbayarea.com/news/ sports/Reality-Check-NFL-Player-Arrests-on-Rise-276411461.html.

Bureau of Justice Statistics. "Arrest Data Analysis Tool." http://www.bjs. gov/index.cfm?ty=datool&surl=/arrests/index.cfm.

CBS New York. 2014. "Feminist Group Flies Banner over MetLife Stadium Calling for Commissioner Goodell's Resignation." September 14. http://newyork.cbslocal.com/2014/09/14/feminist-group-flies-banner-over-metlife-stadium-calling-for-commissioner-goodells-resignation/.

Centers for Disease Control and Prevention. 2003. National Center for Injury Prevention and Control, "Costs of Intimate Partner Violence against Women in the United States." http://www.cdc.gov/violen ceprevention/pdf/IPVBook-a.pdf.

Davis, M. E., C. Ericson, C. Tompkins, and M. Raskin. 2005. "Family Violence and Social Indicators Project." http://www.fact.virginia.gov/ pdfs/George_Mason_Final_Report.pdf.

Davis, W. II. 2014. "A Numbers Game: Making an NFL Roster" *Huff Post Sports* Blog, August 28. http://www.huffingtonpost.com/ wade-davis-jr-a-numbers-game-making-an-nfl-roster_b_5731630. html.

DoSomething.Org. 2015. "11 facts about Domestic and Dating Violence." https://www.dosomething.org/facts/11-facts-about-domestic-and-dating-violence.

FBI Uniform Crime Reports. 2010. "Crime in the United States: Arrests Males: by Age, 2010." http://www.fbi.gov/about-us/cjis/ucr/crime-in-the-u.s/2010/crime-in-the-u.s.-2010/tables/10tbl39.xls.

Goodman, L. A., M. Dutton, and L. Bennett. 2000. "Predicting Repeat Abuse among Arrested Batterers Use of the Danger Assessment Scale in the Criminal Justice System." *Journal of Interpersonal Violence* 15: 63–74.

Hall, A. 2014. "Is Domestic Violence a Bigger Problem than We Realize? Illustrates How Deep the Problem Goes." *Huffington Post*, November 19. http://www.huffingtonpost.com/2014/11/19/domes tic-violence-infographic_n_6181058.html.

Hirschel, D. 2008. "Domestic Violence Cases: What Research Shows about Arrest and Dual Arrest Rates." https://www.ncjrs.gov/pdffiles1/nij/222679.pdf

Irwin, N. 2014. "What the Numbers Show about N.F.L. Player Arrests." *New York Times*, September 12. http://www.nytimes.com/2014/09/13/upshot/what-the-numbers-show-about-nfl-player-arrests.html?hp&action=click&pgtype=Homepage&version=Hp Sum&module=second-column-region&region=top-news&WT.nav=top-news&abt=0002&abg=1&_r=0.

Iyengar, R. 2007. "Does the Certainty of Arrest Reduce Domestic Violence? Evidence from Mandatory and Recommended Arrest Laws." Working paper No. 13186. Cambridge, MA: National Bureau of Economic Research. http://www.nber.org/papers/w13186.pdf.

Morris, B. 2014. "The Rate of Domestic-Violence Arrests among NFL Players." *FiveThirtyEightSports*, July 13. http://fivethirtyeight.com/datalab/the-rate-of-domestic-violence-arrests-among-nfl-players/.

National Organization of Women. 2014. "NOW Calls for Roger Goodell's Resignation, Appointment of Independent Investigator" September 9. http://now.org/media-center/press-release/now-calls-for-roger-goodells-resignation-appointment-of-independent-investigator/.

Nixon, J. "NFL Player Arrests: Facts vs. Fiction, 2015." Jeff Nixon sports blog. http://jeffnixon.sportsblog.com/posts/1786352/nfl_player_arrest_database.html.

Olbermann, K. Quoted in *SB Nation*. "Keith Olbermann: 'Roger Goodell Must Resign' over Ray Rice Punishment." August 2, 2014, http://www.sbnation.com/nfl/2014/8/2/5962037/keith-olbermann-roger-goodell-ray-rice-punishment.

Powell-Morse, A. 2014. "The Unofficial 2014 NFL Player Census." BestTicketsBlog, September 23. http://www.besttickets.com/blog/nfl-player-census-2014/.

Simpson, I. 2014. "Violent U.S. Crime Drops Again, Reaches 1970s Level: FBI." *Reuters*, November 10. http://www.reuters.com/article/2014/11/10/us-usa-crime-fbi-idUSKCN0IU1UM20141110.

Sessler, M. 2012. "NFL increases offseason roster limit to 90 players" NFL, April 23. http://www.nfl.com/news/story/09000d5d82889dda/article/nfl-increases-offseason-roster-limit to 90-players.

The Week. 2014. "NFL Commissioner Roger Goodell on Ray Rice Punishment: 'I Didn't Get It Right.'" August 28. http://theweek.com/speedreads/447218/nfl-commissioner-roger-goodell-ray-rice-punishment-didnt-right.

Truman, J. L., and M. Planty. 2012. "Criminal Victimization, 2011." Bureau of Justice Statistics, http://www.bjs.gov/content/pub/pdf/cv11.pdf.

USA Today. 2000-2014. "NFL Player Arrests." http://www.usatoday.com/sports/nfl/arrests/.

US Bureau of Justice Statistics. 2012. "Intimate Partner Violence, 1993–2010." http://www.bjs.gov/content/pub/pdf/ipv9310.pdf.

US Census Bureau. "Census Bureau Regions and Divisions with State FIPS Codes" Accessed 2015. http://www2.census.gov/geo/pdfs/maps-data/maps/reference/us_regdiv.pdf.

US Department of Justice 2013 in CBSNEWS. "Justice Department: Violence against women fell 64% over decade." March 7. http://www.cbsnews.com/news/justice-dept-violence-against-women-fell-64-over-decade/.

Vinik, D. 2014. "If Roger Goodell Saw the Tape, He Needs to Step Down as NFL Commissioner." *New Republic*, September 10. http://www.newrepublic.com/article/119399/goodell-should-resign-if-nfl-saw-second-tape-ray-rice-monday.

Wilner, B. 2014. "Roger Goodell Admits Mistakes in Domestic Violence Cases, Won't Resign." *Denver Post Sports*, September. http://www.denverpost.com/broncos/ci_26566582/roger-goodell-make-first-public-statement-nfl-partner.

World Health Organization. 2013. "Violence against Women: A Global Health Problem of Epidemic Proportions." http://www.who.int/mediacentre/news/releases/2013/violence_against_women_20130620/en/.

Table 3-1. Domestic-Violence Arrest Rates in the NFL, 2000–14							
Year	2000	2001	2002	2003	2004	2000-04*	
Number of Players	1,777	1,786	1,885	1,889	1,927	9,264	
Number of Domestic-Violence Arrests	5	8	4	4	2	23	
Domestic-Violence Arrest Rate^	2.8	4.5	2.1	2.1	1.0	2.5	
Year	2005	2006	2007	2008	2009	2005-09*	
Number of Players	1,917	1,905	1,940	1,907	1,954	9,623	
Number of Domestic-Violence Arrests	10	10	5	10	4	39	
Domestic-Violence Arrest Rate^	5.2	5.2	2.6	5.2	2.0	4.1	
Year	2010	2011	2012	2013	2014	2010-14*	2000-14*
Number of Players	1,926	1,910	1,938	1,911	1,936	9,621	28,508
Number of Domestic-Violence Arrests	6	3	3	6	5	23	85
Domestic-Violence Arrest Rate^	3.1	1.6	1.5	3.1	2.6	2.4	3.0

* annualized rate   ^ per 1,000 players

Table 3-2. Number of Domestic-Violence Arrests among NFL Players by Month of Arrest, in Five-Year Periods, 2000–14				
	Five-Year Periods			
	2000-04	2005-09	2010-14	2000-14
Month of Arrest				
January	1	3	3	7
February	1	4	2	7
March	3	7	1	11
April	0	4	2	6
May	4	3	3	10
June	4	6	1	11
July	4	2	1	7
August	2	2	2	6
September	1	3	2	6
October	1	4	2	7
November	0	1	3	4
December	2	0	1	3
Totals	23	39	23	85
off-season months				

	Number of Domestic-Violence Arrests	Domestic-Violence Arrest Rate*	Incidence Rate Ratio	95% CI
Table 3-3. Statistical Summary of Domestic-Violence Arrest Rates by Age and Player Position, 2010–14				
Age Group (years)				
24 and younger	8	2.2	Index Reference	
25 to 27	10	3.2	1.4	0.5, 4.1
28+	5	1.7	0.8	0.2, 2.7
Six-Group Position				
Offensive linemen	0	0	N/A	
Defensive linemen	5	3.4	1.4	0.3, 9.0
Offensive backs	3	2.4	Index Reference	
Defensive backs	12	3.7	1.5	0.4, 8.4
Receivers	3	1.8	0.7	0.1, 5.4
Kickers	0	0	N/A	

* per 1,000 players

Table 3-4. Number of Domestic-Violence Arrests by NFL Teams, 2010–14			
	Five-Year Periods			
Team	2000-04	2005-09	2010-14	2000-14
Broncos	4	6	1	11
Dolphins	2	2	3	7
Cardinals	3	0	2	5
Seahawks	0	3	2	5
Steelers	0	4	1	5
Bengals	3	1	0	4
Bucs	2	1	1	4
Chiefs	2	2	0	4
Titans	0	4	0	4
Falcons	0	2	1	3
Packers	0	1	2	3
Patriots	2	1	0	3
Vikings	0	1	2	3
Chargers	0	2	0	2
Colts	1	1	0	2
Jets	0	0	2	2
Lions	0	1	1	2
Panthers	1	0	1	2
Raiders	0	2	0	2
Rams	0	2	0	2
Ravens	1	0	1	2
Saints	0	1	1	2
Texans	1	1	0	2
49ers	0	0	1	1
Browns	0	1	0	1
Cowboys	0	0	1	1
Redskins	1	0	0	1
Bills	0	0	0	0
Eagles	0	0	0	0
Jaguars	0	0	0	0
Totals	23	39	23	85

Table 3-5. Number of Domestic-Violence Arrests by Birthplace (Region) and Five-Year Periods, 2000–14

| | Five-Year Periods | | | | | | | |
| | 2000–04 | | 2005–09 | | 2010–14 | | 2000–14 | |
Birthplace (Region)	N	%	N	%	N	%	N	%
Midwest	4	17.4	6	15.8	2	8.7	12	14.3
Northeast	0	0.0	2	5.3	3	13.0	5	6.0
South	15	65.2	26	68.4	15	65.2	56	66.7
West	4	17.4	4	10.5	3	13.0	11	13.1
Totals^	23	100.0	38	100.0	23	100.0	84	100.0

^One player arrested for domestic violence was born outside of the United States.

Note: In 2013, about 51.9% of all NFL players were born in states from the Southern region of the United States

Driving under the Influence (DUI) Arrests: NFL Players versus the US General Population

• • •

Driving under the influence (DUI) involving alcohol is a large public-health problem impacting thousands of people each year. A 2013 US Department of Transportation report found that in the United States in 2013 alone, there were more than ten thousand deaths from alcohol-impaired driving crashes that involved drivers (65 percent), other occupants (27 percent), and nonoccupants (8 percent) (US. Department of Transportation 2013). The report also found that more than 30 percent of all motor-vehicle fatalities in the United States involve intoxicated drivers. Blincoe et al. (2014) found that nearly three hundred thousand people are injured in car crashes involving drunk drivers. Nearly twice as many fatal car crashes involving drunk drivers occur in males compared to females (FBI 2011). Nearly one out of every four drunk drivers is an individual who is in the age range from twenty-one to twenty-five years (US Department of Transportation 2013).

In all fifty states, driving while impaired is defined as occurring when there is a blood alcohol concentration (BAC) level of at least 0.08 g/dl. According to the Centers for Disease Control (2011), in 2010 there were 479 episodes of alcohol-impaired driving per 1,000 adults aged eighteen and over. In all, there were about 112 million episodes of alcohol-impaired driving that year. The Centers for Disease Control (2011) found that males in the age range of twenty-one to thirty-four years, the same age range as about 98 percent of all NFL players, account for more than 80 percent of these episodes. It also estimates that even before their first arrest, drivers have driven while drunk about eighty times. On an economic level, motor-vehicle crashes account for nearly $60 billion in costs, and 84 percent of these expenditures involve drivers or nonoccupants with elevated BAC levels (Blincoe et al. 2014).

DUI arrests among NFL players are sometimes reported in the sports and other news media. Several highly publicized incidents involving NFL players have resulted in fatalities to motor-vehicle occupants and pedestrians (Glasspiegel 2014). One DUI-related accident involving an NFL player resulted in the death of a teammate (Ackerman 2012, Dixon 2012). During the most recent fifteen-year period, several NFL players have been convicted of manslaughter related to DUI charges and have served significant jail time (Ackerman 2012). Nevertheless, these incidents are not necessarily reflective of a DUI epidemic among NFL players, nor do they indicate that DUI is "sustained and pervasive" in the NFL, as one media report has stated (e.g., Glasspiegel 2014).

This chapter examines the incidence of DUI arrests among NFL regular-season players and compares these rates to the incidence in the US general population. I computed age-specific DUI arrest rates and compared them to the general population over a four-year study period, 2010 through 2013.

METHODS

Rates, whether related to disease, arrests, or death, require a valid numerator and denominator. Typically, these rates are expressed per some specific unit of time. When a special population, like NFL players, is being compared to a general population, several factors need to be considered. Perhaps the most important factor is to select a general population that resembles the players in ways that make the comparisons meaningful. For example, NFL players consist of males only, and they are generally in the age range of twenty to forty-four years, although only a small percentage of players exceed thirty-five years of age. In choosing a population to compare to NFL players, one priority would be selecting males in this same age range.

Because both gender (Insurance Institute for Highway Safety 2013) and age (Substance Abuse and Mental Health Services Administration 2011) are known to be associated with DUI arrest rates, the exclusion of women and men over the age of forty-four is required for a meaningful general-population comparison. Also, instead of comparing all subjects within a wide age span, like between the ages of twenty and forty-four, an effort should be made to conduct age-specific analyses within narrower age ranges. This will help reduce variation related to the distribution of ages within a larger range. Time is another factor to be considered. If DUI arrest rates among NFL players are being compared for the period 2010 through 2013, researchers should select DUI arrest and population statistics only from these years.

Another principle in computing rates is that the individuals in the numerator must be a subset of the population in the denominator. As an example, if the denominator is based on regular-season NFL players, DUI arrestees should not be counted if they played in the preseason only. Finally, the definition of the disease or problem being studied—in this case DUI arrests—has to be defined as consistently as possible across the populations being compared. The following sections describe the methodology used in this study to derive the numerators and denominators.

NFL Players

The methods I used to calculate the numerator, denominator, and DUI arrest rates for NFL players are described below.

Numerator

I obtained the numerator for DUI arrest rates among players from NFL arrest records published online by *USA Today* and the *San Diego Union-Tribune* (*USA Today* 2010-13, *San Diego Union-Tribune* 2010-13). The two databases are largely the same, although one DUI arrest included in this study is identified in the *San Diego Union-Tribune* database but excluded from that of *USA Today*. After confirming this case using several reputable news publications, I added it to the DUI numerator for NFL players. The remainder of this chapter refers to the *USA Today* database only, plus the one DUI case that was missed. I identified all DUI arrests of NFL players that occurred during the four-year period from 2010 through 2013. I included only arrests that occurred among regular-season NFL players during any of the four study years, consistent with the way the denominator is computed (as described in the next paragraph). I analyzed the arrests by year of occurrence (2010, 2011, 2012, and 2013) and calculated players' ages according to the dates of their arrests. I used a total of five age groups: ages twenty to twenty-four, ages twenty-five to twenty-nine, ages thirty to thirty-four, ages thirty-five to thirty-nine, and ages forty to forty-four. These age groups cover every NFL player during the study period except for one. This was a forty-six-year-old player who was not arrested for a DUI, so I dropped him from the analyses. In addition to encompassing virtually all NFL players, these age groups are the same ones the US Census Bureau uses to aggregate the US population in published arrest reports, as well as DUI and other statistics published by the FBI.

DENOMINATOR

Based on the number of regular-season players during each of the four study years, I obtained the denominator for DUI arrest rates among NFL players using a combination of NFL team rosters (NFL, 2010–13, Team Rosters) and game logs (NFL, 2010–13, Game Logs) published on the NFL website. In contrast, DUI arrests published in the *USA Today* "NFL Player Arrests" database sometimes include players who do not make a regular-season NFL roster. Although it is possible to derive a denominator for preseason players who do not play in the regular season, for a number of reasons this is difficult and requires more data-management resources. Therefore, this study focuses solely on players who played in the regular seasons of interest. While this strategy facilitates denominator and rate calculations for DUI and other kinds of arrests, it excludes a number of preseason (only) players who are included in the *USA Today* arrests database. I discuss this methodology further later on.

General Population

The next calculations I look at relate to the general population.

Numerator

Each year, the FBI publishes the Uniform Crime Report (UCR), which contains the number of arrests in the United States for a wide range of crimes (FBI 2010–13). One arrest category included in this report is "Driving under the influence." The UCR reports present the number of DUI arrests categorized by a number of age groups, which are the same five age groups previously described. The UCR numbers are based on a large subset of the US population derived from the number of agencies that report arrests to the FBI. Typically, about 75 to 80 percent of the entire US population is covered in these reports, and the exact size of the underlying population is documented in the FBI reports.

Denominator

I based the denominator for the general population on total-population statistics compiled and reported by the US Bureau of the Census (2010). As mandated by the US Constitution, the census is conducted every ten years. The US Census Bureau also releases in-between-census population estimates for each intervening year. The methodology for these "in-between" estimates is detailed elsewhere (US Census Bureau, no date given). For this study, I obtained the total US population statistics for males in each of the aforementioned five age groups for each of the four study years.

Because the UCR statistics are based on a population that is 75 to 80 percent of the entire US population, I made an adjustment to the US Census Bureau numbers prior to calculating the DUI arrest rates—that is, I trimmed the total population numbers in proportion to the available UCR numbers. For example, suppose that the total US population for a year of interest was three hundred million people, and during this same year, UCR statistics were available for 80 percent of the population. I would reduce the total population numbers by 20 percent, or 60 million, to 240 million. I would apply this same adjustment to each of the five age groups, reducing each by 20 percent. I describe possible limitations associated with this approach in the "Discussion" section.

In all, I calculated five age-specific DUI rates for NFL players and the general population for each study year. In addition, I computed an annual rate that is a weighted average of all five age-specific rates for each year. I calculated a total of twenty age-specific DUI arrest rates plus four annual rates for both the general population and NFL players. The arrest rates I present in this chapter reflect the number of DUI arrests per thousand people in the general population, or per thousand NFL regular-season players, computed on a per-year basis.

RESULTS
I have already presented background statistics for all regular-season players included in this study in table 1-1 in chapter 1.

Table 4-1 contains all numerator and denominator data for the general population, DUI arrest rates for each age group and study year, and annual DUI arrest rates. In each study year, DUI arrest rates per thousand people in the general population are highest in the twenty- to twenty-four-year age group, ranging from 15.3 in 2013 to 20.1 in 2010. As age increases, there is a consistent decline in DUI arrest rates. In 2010, for example, DUI arrest rates per thousand people in the general population decreased from 20.1 in the twenty- to twenty-four-year age group to 18.4, 14.0, 11.0, and 9.5 in the next four older age groups, respectively. Within each general-population age group, DUI arrest rates tend to decline each year, with the exception of 2012, when rates rise slightly from the previous year. For example, in the twenty- to twenty-four-year age group, DUI arrest rates per thousand people are 20.1 in 2010 and drop to 16.7 in 2011. In 2012, DUI arrest rates rise slightly to 17.2 per thousand people in this age range but then drop to 15.3 in 2012. These patterns of DUI arrest rates in the general population in relation to age group and year are very consistent. When the five age groups are collapsed into an annual DUI arrest rate, the general population averages 14.7, 12.4, 13.0 and 11.9 per thousand people in 2010 through 2013, respectively.

As shown in table 4-2, between 2010 and 2013, there were 1,926, 1,910, 1,938, and 1,911 regular-season NFL players, respectively. I used these numbers as the denominators in the DUI arrest-rate calculations for NFL players. Of those who played in at least one regular season between 2010 and 2013, there were a total of fifty-six DUI arrests among fifty-four NFL players; two players had two DUI arrests each. These fifty-four players had a mean age at arrest of 25.7 years, with a median age of 25. During the four study years, there were eighteen, seven, eighteen, and thirteen total DUI arrests among regular-season NFL players, respectively. DUI annual arrest rates per 1,000 NFL players average 9.4, 3.7, 9.3, and 6.8 in 2010 through 2013, respectively.

The age and time patterns obtained for DUI arrest rates in the general population are different for NFL players. This is, at least in part, due to a difference in the age distributions of the general population versus those of the players. Unlike the general population, only 169, or about 2 percent, of all regular-season NFL players are thirty-five years of age or older. Within this relatively small group, there was only one arrest (in 2011) among players over the age of thirty-five during all four study years combined. Hence, seven of the eight age-specific DUI arrest rates among NFL players are zero in the two older age groups during all four study years. In contrast, general-population denominators in the thirty-five-and-older age group are large, averaging roughly eight million in the age group during the four study years. DUI arrest rates in the two older age groups within the general population are in the range of 7.8 to 11.0 per 1,000. Because DUI is a relatively rare event in the NFL and the denominators are small, arrest rates among NFL players are usually zero in the two older age groups.

DUI annual arrest rates for NFL players during 2012 and 2013 follow the same age and time patterns observed in the general population when only the three younger age groups are considered—that is, DUI arrest rates in 2012 and 2013 are lower for twenty-five to twenty-nine-year-olds compared to twenty- to twenty-four-year-olds, and then drop further within thirty- to thirty-four-year-old players. Also, like the general population, DUI arrest rates declined among NFL players between 2012 and 2013. DUI arrest rates for NFL players in 2010 and 2011 are inconsistent with respect to age and time.

A summary of the DUI arrest rates for the general population and NFL is shown in table 4-3. The general-population rates are higher than those for NFL players in nineteen of twenty age-specific groups during the four study years. The only exception is in 2011, when 22.2 per 1,000 NFL players were arrested for DUI in the thirty-five to thirty-nine year age group, compared to 9.4 for the general population. However, the NFL rate is based on only one player who was arrested for DUI that year in that age range.

With respect to annual DUI arrest rates, those for the general population are higher than those for NFL players in all four study years. For 2010 through 2013, the total DUI arrest rates in the general population are 14.7, 12.4, 13.0, and 11.9 per 1,000 people, compared to 9.4, 3.7, 9.3, and 6.3 per 1,000 NFL players, respectively.

Discussion

Comparisons of the DUI arrest rates between the general population and NFL regular-season players reveal that NFL players have lower rates. This is evident in nineteen of twenty of the age-specific comparisons over a four-year study period as well as in the annual rates that combine the results across the five age groups. General-population results with respect to age and time are fairly consistent, revealing an inverse relationship between age group and DUI arrests. It can thus be assumed that DUI arrest rates decline as age increases. This is a known trend in the general population that has been documented in reports published by the Substance Abuse and Mental Health Services Administration (2011) and serves as a measure of the face validity of comparable results obtained in this study. In addition, general-population DUI arrest rates have declined between 2010 and 2013, although this drop has not been altogether steady each year. Unlike the general population, few NFL players, about 2 percent, are thirty-five years and older. Hence, there are limited data in this study about NFL players in the two older age groups. In contrast, within the three younger age groups, there are sufficient NFL data to observe patterns that lead to meaningful conclusions. During the final two years of the study, 2012 and 2013, there appears to be the same inverse relationship between age group and DUI arrests among NFL players as is observed in the general population.

Despite the sparseness and inconsistency of the NFL data, the results presented in this chapter cast doubt on published media reports making claims such as this: "The NFL has a sustained, pervasive, drunk driving problem" (Glasspiegel 2014). The finding of lower DUI rates among NFL players than in the general population, however, does not minimize the relevance and significance of drinking and driving as a problem for society in general, and the league and its players specifically. Moreover, the data presented in this chapter do not address the relative damage and loss associated with DUI in the two populations. It remains unknown, for example, whether, on average, DUIs among NFL players cause more (or less) physical harm to drivers, occupants, and/or innocent bystanders than DUIs involving the general population. Another limitation is that data for this chapter cannot be used to address relative blood alcohol content (BAC) values in DUI arrestees in the NFL relative to the general population. Nor are data available to determine average DUI-related jail time and other possible negative impacts on careers, families, and teams/coworkers. Even if losses and damages associated with DUI arrests are equivalent in the NFL and the general population, these impacts can be considerable and can affect players and innocent bystanders in a multitude of terrible ways for lengthy periods of time—even a lifetime.

It is probably naïve to think that DUIs, and DUI arrests, can be completely eliminated in the NFL. Nevertheless, elimination could be the goal for the league and the NFL Players Association. Additional educational programs and stiffer penalties are measures the NFL can consider in dealing with this very serious problem. According to league officials, mandatory suspensions for first-time DUIs are being considered (Schrotenboer 2013). A number of recent drunk-driving incidents among league executives (Martin 2013), including that of an NFL team owner (Disis and Evans 2014), cannot be viewed in isolation from those of the players given the owners' influential roles. This particular DUI arrest of an NFL team owner was especially troubling because it was also determined that the owner had oxycodone, hydrocodone, and alprazolam in his system at the time of the arrest (Disis and Evans 2014).

Attempting to compare NFL arrest rates for any crime to those of the general US population is methodologically and statistically challenging and generally requires advanced professional training in biostatistics and epidemiology. This is not a casual undertaking that can be readily tackled by individuals without relevant public-health training. Several published Internet articles, while well intended, have been seriously flawed and have sometimes reached conclusions that are erroneous.

One popular sports website posted an article in 2013 that purported to compare rates of DUI among NFL players to those of the US adult-male general population for the year 2010. (Fischer-Baum 2013) That paper used the *San Diego Union-Tribune* NFL arrests database (*San Diego Union-Tribune* updated regularly). The author began with an estimation of the total number of NFL players in 2010 that was achieved by multiplying fifty-three (the number of regular-season roster spots) by thirty-two (the number of NFL teams). This comes to 1,696 players. Fischer-Baum 2013) While it is true that each of the thirty-two teams has fifty-three roster spots during the regular season, the sample of players on each team is dynamic, not static. There are free-agent signings, releases, trades, Injured Reserve List placements, suspensions, and many other transactions that result in roster changes. In fact, the data presented in this book (see table 1-1) indicate that more than 1,900 different players have played at least one regular-season game in the NFL each year since 2010, which gives us a number closer to sixty players per team. (As I will go on to explain, regular-season roster size is not an appropriate denominator for these kinds of computations in any case.) This same author did not use age-specific categories to compute DUI arrest rates. Instead, it appears that the total number of DUI arrests for every age combined was used as the numerator, and the entire adult-male US population was used as the denominator. The inclusion of males over the age of forty-five in the general-population numerators and denominators is inappropriate for a comparison with NFL players.

This is not the only instance of lay calculations of DUI arrest rates that appear on the Internet and in other publications (e.g., *New York Times* 2014). Moreover, some of the online articles containing questionable methods and conclusions are being cited in other publications (e.g., Schapiro 2014). Hence, a "snowball" effect of published misinformation has developed on this topic.

It may come as a surprise to some people that a number of players listed in the *USA Today* and *San Diego Union-Tribune* databases as DUI arrestees never played in an NFL regular season. The following is a summary of one player's real career history in the NFL. This player was listed in both of these arrest databases for DUI in 2015. Here are some facts about this specific player:

- He has no official NFL statistics.
- He is not listed as a current or historical player on the NFL or ESPN websites.
- An NFL team signed him as an undrafted free agent in June 2014 but later cut him.
- A second NFL team signed him several months later, and he became a member of its practice squad.
- He signed a reserve/future contract with a third NFL team in January 2015 but was released two months later, after being arrested for a DUI.

From all accounts, this player never played a single down in a regular or even preseason NFL game. Nevertheless, he is listed in the popular arrest databases for NFL players. In fact, there are a number of players with these kinds of NFL careers who get arrested but still appear in the online NFL arrest databases. Anyone who uses these databases and attempts to calculate a rate for any kind of arrest would be obliged to include regular and preseason player status in their computations. If they fail to do this, their rate calculations could be subject to substantial error.

A number of sports writers have used the fifty-three-man regular-season team roster number to derive denominators in their arrest-rate calculations, and I've already explained why this is generally inappropriate. The player just described, and others like him, would never appear on any regular-season roster. At the beginning of training camp, preseason rosters are populated with a maximum of ninety players on each NFL team, per NFL rules (Davis 2014). This number is still an inadequate denominator when using the two popular online arrest databases. If an author includes a player who virtually never played an NFL game in his or her numerator for DUI arrests, then the denominator would have to consist of any player who had signed an NFL contract. From a practical perspective, this latter number would be difficult to obtain. NFL transaction pages found on websites like those of NFL and ESPN (NFL, Transactions, 2010–13; ESPN, Transactions) display hundreds and perhaps thousands of player signings each year. Any rate that uses the online arrest databases for its numerator but does not use all players that sign with an NFL team as its denominator will be incorrect. The use of regular season roster size, or even preseason roster size for this purpose, will result in denominators that are understated, and hence, rates that are inflated.

This chapter contains DUI arrest rate calculations that include only players who actually played in at least one regular season during the study's years of interest. Hence, players like the one just described in detail would not be counted as a DUI arrest for purposes of this chapter. This method should not be taken as an attempt to ignore players who may have more marginal or less successful NFL careers. They may be very talented players who have worked very hard to even be considered by NFL teams. Nor is this exclusion an unfair minimizing of DUI arrests and arrest rates in the NFL. Simply put, the exclusion of these players from the analysis is a practical consideration that helps with the computation of meaningful arrest rates.

There have been other scientific analyses that compare rates of arrest and include a number of violent crimes such as assaults, domestic violence, rape, kidnapping, and homicide among NFL players versus the general population (e.g., Blumstein and Benedict 1999). In these analyses, race is a critical stratification variable because there are purported to be large differences in arrest rates between African Americans and whites on some of the crimes that are investigated. Interestingly, and consistent with the findings of this chapter, this prior research also observes lower arrest rates among NFL players versus the general population. According to these authors, "NFL [arrest] rates are less than half the general population rates for both whites and blacks" (Blumstein and Benedict 1999, 14).

Obviously, some NFL players are large in physical size and weight, and as such there could be misconceptions among individuals regarding drinking and its impact on blood alcohol levels. Even at 240 pounds, about the average for NFL players, five alcoholic drinks can result in a BAC level of 0.08 or higher. Players who generally weigh less, like wide receivers and safeties, can exceed the maximum BAC by consuming four or fewer alcoholic drinks. Moreover, BAC could be influenced by fatigue and illness (DrinkingAndDriving.Org 2008–14). Drivers with BAC levels as low as 0.04 would not be considered legally drunk but could be noticeably affected in their ability to drive. Moreover, there are criminal penalties in some states if someone is found to be driving at BAC levels that are above 0.04 (DrinkingAndDriving.Org 2008–14).

The findings in this chapter are subject to a number of important limitations and qualifications. For one, the *USA Today* arrests database may not include every arrest. Moreover, an arrest does not necessarily result in a conviction, and again, in the United States, there is a presumption of innocence for all arrestees. As one reporter notes, "The data set [*USA Today*] is imperfect; after all, it depends on news media outlets finding out about every time a third-string offensive lineman is pulled over for driving drunk, and so some arrests may well fall through the cracks. Moreover, arrests are included even if charges are dropped or the player is found not guilty, so it presumably includes legal run-ins in which the player did nothing wrong" (*The New York Times* 2014).

Based on my own work, I do believe that the online arrest databases are complete, or close to it. Nevertheless, some arrests could be missed.

It is also likely that there are people who commit crimes and are never caught or arrested.

The adjustment made to the general-population denominators used in this chapter is consistent with the respective sizes of the underlying FBI populations. It is unknown, however, whether the individuals covered by the FBI arrest databases, typically about 75 to 80 percent of the entire US population, are proportional within the age groups that are analyzed in this chapter. In other words, while the percentage and number of the US population missed by the UCR reports is known, it is unknown whether these exclusions occur in the same proportion for each age range. I made this assumption in the calculations used in this chapter.

It is possible that NFL players drive less on their own during football-playing months when they are busy playing football and traveling with their teams on airplanes and team buses. If this is true, then players' risk of driving under the influence may be reduced during these periods. This potential reduced exposure to driving may help to explain lower DUI rates among NFL players compared to the general population. Additional research is required to systematically address this possibility.

Another potential limitation of this chapter has to do with the manner in which DUI arrest rates are defined and counted in the two data sources used in this study to identify arrestees (the *USA Today* "NFL Player Arrests" database and the FBI's UCR reports). There is, however, some reasonable likelihood that the two organizations are consistent regarding how DUI arrests are defined. This is because every state in the United States uses the same standard for defining impaired driving (i.e., a BAC level of at least 0.08 g/dl). While actual rates of arrests may differ from one geographic location to another, the use of a single BAC level across the country could add some consistency to how DUI arrests are defined and counted.

Concluding Remarks

This chapter has documented a consistently lower rate of DUI arrests among NFL players compared to the US general population for males in the appropriate age range. These results do not in any way minimize the problem and significance of DUI arrests among NFL players. Everyone associated with the NFL must aggressively seek ways to minimize the problem of DUI. Comments made by sports writers and other publication media referring to a pervasive DUI problem among NFL players, however, may require qualification in light of these findings. The league, the NFLPA, and the players themselves must work as hard as possible to reduce or eliminate DUI altogether within their ranks.

REFERENCES

Ackerman, M. 2012. "Can the NFL Tackle Its DUI Problem?" *Fix*, December 10. http://www.thefix.com/content/nfl-tackles-dui-problem91013.

BlackDemographics.com. "2014 Census Black Population Estimates." http://blackdemographics.com/population/.

Blincoe, L. J., T. R. Miller, E. Zaloshnja, and B. A. Lawrence. 2014. "The Economic and Societal Impact of Motor Vehicle Crashes, 2010." Report no. DOT HS 812 013. Washington, DC: National Highway Traffic Safety Administration. http://www-nrd.nhtsa.dot.gov/pubs/812013.pdf.

Blumstein, A., and J. Benedict. 1999. "Criminal Violence of NFL Players Compared to the General Population." *Chance* 12 (3).

Centers for Disease Control and Prevention. 2010. "Vital Signs: Alcohol-Impaired Driving among Adults—United States." *Morbidity and Mortality Weekly Report (MMWR)* 60 (39): 1351–56.

Davis, W II. 2014. "A Numbers Game: Making an NFL Roster." *Huff Post Sports*, August 28. http://www.huffingtonpost.com/wade-davis-jr/a-numbers-game-making-an-nfl-roster_b_5731630.html.

Disis, J., and T. Evans. 2014. "Colt Owner Jim Irsay's DUI Arrest Video Is Released." *USA Today*, October 17. http://www.usatoday.com/story/sports/nfl/colts/2014/10/17/jim-irsay-dui-arrest-video-indianapolis-colts-owner/17439325/.

Dixon, S. 2012. "NFL Drunk Driving Safety Net: Death of Jerry Brown, Arrest Of Josh Brent Raises Questions." *Huff Post Sports*, December 10. http://www.huffingtonpost.com/2012/12/10/nfl-drunk-driving-cowboys-josh-brent_n_2273727.html.

DrinkingAndDriving.Org. 2008–2014. "Blood Alcohol Content." http://www.drinkinganddriving.org/Articles/blood-alcohol-content.html.

ESPN. 2010–2013. "NFL Transactions." http://m.espn.go.com/nfl/transactions.

Federal Bureau of Investigation (FBI) Uniform Crime Rates. 2010. "Crime in the United States" Table 39, Males by Age, 2010–2013. http://www.fbi.gov/about-us/cjis/ucr/crime-in-the-u.s/2010/crime-in-the-u.s.-2010/tables/10tbl39.xls.

———. 2011. "Crime in the United States" Table 39, Males by Age, 2010–2013. 2011. http://www.fbi.gov/about-us/cjis/ucr/crime-in-the-u.s/2011/crime-in-the-u.s.-2011/tables/table-39.

———. 2012. "Crime in the United States" Table 39, Males by Age, 2010–2013. http://www.fbi.gov/about-us/cjis/ucr/crime-in-the-u.s/2012/crime-in-the-u.s.-2012/tables/39tabledatadecoverviewpdf

———. 2013. "Crime in the United States" Table 39, Males by Age, 2010–2013. http://www.fbi.gov/aboutus/cjis/ucr/crime-in-the-us/2013/crime-in-the-u.s.-2013/tables/39tabledatacoverviewpdf

Fischer-Baum R. 2013 "What do arrest data really say about NFL players and crime?" Deadspin, http://deadspin.com/what-do-arrests-data-really-say-about-nfl-players-and-c-733301399

Glasspiegel, R. 2014. "The NFL Has a Sustained, Pervasive, Drunk Driving Problem." BigLead, May 30. http://thebiglead.com/2014/05/30/the-nfl-has-a-sustained-pervasive-drunk-driving-problem/.

Insurance Institute for Highway Safety, Highway Loss Data Institute. 2013. "General Statistics: Gender." http://www.iihs.org/iihs/topics/t/general-statistics/fatalityfacts/gender.

Martin, J. 2013. "DUI Epidemic? NFL Player Arrests Up 75 percent from Last Year." Martin Law Firm blog, August 16. http://www.jbmartinlaw.com/blogs/legal/bid/117789/DUI-Epidemic-NFL-Player-Arrests-Up-75-from-Last-Year.

Milhoces, G. 2014. "Annual Diversity Report Gives NFL 'B' For Racial, Gender Hiring Practices." *USA Today*, September 17. http://www.usatoday.com/story/sports/nfl/2014/09/17/racial-and-gender-report-card-grade-b-diverstiy/15780865/

New York Times, the Upshot. 2014. "What the Numbers Show about N.F.L. Player Arrests." *New York Times*, September 12. http://www.nytimes.com/2014/09/13/upshot/what-the-numbers-show-about-nfl-player-arrests.html?_r=0&abt=0002&abg=1.

NFL. 2010–2013. "Game Logs." NFL. http://www.nfl.com/player/elimanning/2505996/gamelogs.

NFL. 2010–2014. "NFL Transactions." http://www.nfl.com/transactions.

NFL. 2010–2014. "Team Rosters." NFL. http://www.nfl.com/players/search?category=team&playerType=current.

San Diego Union-Tribune. 2010-13. "NFL Arrests Database" http://www .utsandiego.com/nfl/arrests-database/.

Schapiro, R. 2014. "NFL Players Are More Likely to Get Arrested for DUI than Domestic Abuse, Assault: Data." *New York Daily News,* September 13. http://www.nydailynews.com/sports/football/ nfl-players-arrested-dui-domestic-abuse-assault-article-1.1938854.

Schrotenboer, B. 2013. "NFL Arrests Persist after Turbulent Offseason." *USA Today* Sports, September 5. http://www.usatoday.com/story /sports/nfl/2013/09/04/arrest-aaron-hernandez-roger-goodell-dui- assault/2764291/.

Substance Abuse and Mental Health Services Administration. 2011. "Results from the 2010 National Survey on Drug Use and Health: Summary of National Findings." HHS publication no. (SMA) 11-4658. Rockville, MD: Substance Abuse and Mental Health Services Administration. http://archive.samhsa.gov/data/ NSDUH/2k10NSDUH/2k10Results.htm#3.1.10.

US Department of Transportation, National Highway Safety Administra- tion. 2013. "Traffic Safety Facts, 2012 Data, Alcohol-Impaired Driving." DOT HS 811 870.

United States Census Bureau. "2010 Age and Sex Composition." http:// factfinder.census.gov/faces/tableservices/jsf/pages/productview. xhtml?src=bkmk.

———. n.d. "Population Estimates." http://www.census.gov/popest/data/ intercensal/.

USA Today. 2010-13. "NFL Player Arrests." http://www.usatoday.com/ sports/nfl/arrests/.

Table 4-1. Driving under the Influence (DUI) Age-Specific Arrest Rates in the US General Population (Males), 2010-2013						
	Age Group (in years)					
	20-24	25-29	30-34	35-39	40-44	Totals
Number of Arrests for Driving under the Influence (DUI)						
2010	172,458	152,305	109,399	85,279	76,412	595,853
2011	145,034	126,742	94,492	70,195	63,906	500,369
2012	153,920	135,268	102,581	74,345	67,442	533,556
2013	138,863	125,786	97,505	70,755	62,129	495,038
Number of People in the US General Population						
2010	11,073,599	10,663,218	10,053,037	9,993,416	10,400,529	52,183,799
2011	11,308,112	10,755,908	10,280,081	9,760,754	10,462,809	52,567,664
2012	11,546,988	10,840,983	10,491,334	9,714,266	10,457,647	53,051,218
2013	11,678,965	10,959,879	10,681,612	9,785,269	10,359,992	53,465,717
Number of People in Adjusted US (FBI) Population						
2010	8,595,482	8,276,939	7,803,308	7,757,029	8,073,036	40,505,794
2011	8,672,202	8,248,717	7,883,804	7,485,532	8,023,939	40,314,194
2012	8,936,888	8,390,469	8,119,855	7,518,437	8,093,783	41,059,433
2013	9,078,605	8,519,625	8,303,316	7,606,546	8,053,305	41,561,397
DUI Arrest Rates per 1,000 General Population						
2010	20.1	18.4	14.0	11.0	9.5	14.7
2011	16.7	15.4	12.0	9.4	8.0	12.4
2012	17.2	16.1	12.6	9.9	8.3	13.0
2013	15.3	14.8	11.7	9.3	7.7	11.9

Table 4-2. Driving under the Influence (DUI) Age-Specific Arrest Rates among NFL Regular-Season Players, 2010-2013	Age Group (in years)					
	20-24	25-29	30-34	35-39	40-44	Totals
Number of Arrests for Driving under the Influence (DUI)						
2010	4	12	2	0	0	18
2011	0	5	1	1	0	7
2012	9	7	2	0	0	18
2013	7	5	1	0	0	13
Number of NFL Regular-Season Players						
2010	689	893	295	44	4	1,925
2011	693	891	277	45	4	1,910
2012	732	904	259	42	1	1,938
2013	721	908	253	28	1	1,911
DUI Arrest Rates per 1,000 NFL Players						
2010	5.8	13.4	6.8	0.0	0.0	9.4
2011	0.0	5.6	3.6	22.2	0.0	3.7
2012	12.3	7.7	7.7	0.0	0.0	9.3
2013	9.7	5.5	4.0	0.0	0.0	6.8

	Table 4- 3. Summary of Driving Under the Influence (DUI) Age-Specific Arrest Rates in the US Population (Males) and among NFL Players, 2010–13							
		Age Group (in years)						
Year	Group	20-24	25-29	30-34	35-39	40-44	Totals
2010	General Population*	20.1	18.4	14.0	11.0	9.5	14.7
	NFL Players	5.8	13.4	6.8	0.0	0.0	9.4
2011	General Population*	16.7	15.4	12.0	9.4	8.0	12.4
	NFL Players	0.0	5.6	3.6	22.2	0.0	3.7
2012	General Population*	17.2	16.1	12.6	9.9	8.3	13.0
	NFL Players	12.3	7.7	7.7	0.0	0.0	9.3
2013	General Population*	15.3	14.8	11.7	9.3	7.7	11.9
	NFL Players	9.7	5.5	4.0	0.0	0.0	6.8
	* US males						

CHAPTER 5

Arrests among Drafted Underclassmen

• • •

THE COLLECTIVE BARGAINING AGREEMENT (CBA) of 2011, signed between the NFL and the NFL Players Association (NFLPA), has had a profound effect on how college players approach their futures in football and the league. The 2011 CBA went into effect for the first time for the 2012 NFL Draft. Not coincidentally, that was the year when the number of underclassmen who formally announced that they would enter the NFL draft rose from fifty-three and fifty-six players in 2010 and 2011, respectively, to sixty-five. The number increased even more in 2013 and 2014, when seventy-three and ninety-eight underclassmen declared for the draft, respectively.

This large increase was primarily due to the rookie wage scale that was agreed on in the 2011 CBA. This agreement mandates that drafted players remain in their initial rookie contracts for at least three years. In many instances, the teams also had an option for a fourth year, and the team's options for first-round picks could be extended into players' fifth season. The CBA changed how money paid to rookies would be applied to a team's salary cap and the pool of money allocated to pay rookies. This made it impossible for these players to sign contracts containing large bonuses, which did happen in previous years, when rookie pools were unaffected by bonus payouts.

In general, the dollar amount of rookie contracts is significantly less than contracts signed afterward. These postrookie contracts no longer count against rookie pools, and bonus money may also be added. The changes implemented with the 2011 CBA leave a larger pool of money available to veteran players after their rookie contracts expire. The preferred method of earning larger sums of money for players (and their agents) became to conclude rookie contracts as soon as possible, at the youngest age declaring for the NFL draft, sometimes following the junior year in college. In declaring for the draft, these players forfeited their remaining college eligibility.

As a rule, the NFL requires that players entering the draft have been out of high school for at least three years. While attending college is not a requirement to declare for the draft, most NFL players do so to improve their skills and gain valuable playing experience. With all of the pressures and changes associated with playing in the NFL, players' immaturity at this stage of life may cause them to act in ways that result in off-field problems. It is not uncommon for college athletes to be arrested for a range of crimes. While their actual conviction rates may be lower than those of nonathletes (Withers 2010), problems with the law can play a role in some players' NFL careers. There is no research that examines arrests in NFL underclassmen versus comparably drafted players who do graduate from college.

METHODS

I downloaded all NFL arrests that occurred from 2010 to 2014 from the *USA Today* "NFL Player Arrests" database and merged them with my own database, which contains background and football-related data on every individual who played in the NFL's 2010–14 regular seasons. (These players are described in table 1-1.) I identified all players who were drafted between 2010 and 2014 using NFL records.

The main sample for this study includes all underclassmen (UC) within the group of drafted players during the five-year period. As controls, I selected an equal number of drafted players who graduated from college after matching them on year drafted and placement in the draft. From this point forward, I refer to these players as "nonunderclassmen controls," or NUCs. So, if a hypothetical underclassman were drafted as number thirty in 2012, I would randomly select a matched control from the remaining players who was drafted in 2012 and is the closest to being chosen as number thirty. In 2012 and 2014, a large number of underclassmen were drafted in the first round. This made it more difficult to select a control that was drafted immediately before or after the index underclassmen. I selected controls before or after underclassmen blind to any of the players' identities.

I give counts of declared underclassmen and the number and the percentage of players who actually played in the NFL for all five study years.

The background variables include age, height, weight, and position. Draft round and exact placement (i.e., number selected) in the draft are also available. I provide descriptive statistics (i.e., mean, median, standard deviation, minimum, and maximum) for age, height, weight, and draft-pick number. I provide numbers and percentages for position and draft round. I collapsed positions into five groups: offensive linemen, offensive backs, receivers, defensive linemen, and defensive backs. (No kickers are in the UC or NUC samples.) I compared all of these background variables for UCs and NUCs.

I tested continuous background variables using independent t-tests, and I assessed categorical variables for between-group differences using chi-square. I displayed number and type of arrests for UC versus NUC players for the five-year study period.

Because players could have more than one arrest during the study period, I used one significance test to determine whether the *number* of arrests in each group was statistically different. I compared the proportion of players with none versus one or more arrests using a second kind of statistical test for matched pairs. I also compared the players' ages at the time of arrest between the two groups.

RESULTS

A total of 225 underclassmen were drafted into the NFL and played in at least one regular season between 2010 and 2014. I selected an equal number of drafted nonunderclassmen and matched them to underclassmen based on the year they were drafted and selection placement within the draft for a total sample size of 450, or 225 pairs of players.

In 2010, about 85 percent of declared underclassmen were drafted and played in the NFL, compared to 58 percent of underclassmen in 2014. The number of declared underclassmen who did not play in the NFL has risen each year between 2010 and 2014, going from eight to forty-one players.

See table 5-1 for a statistical comparison of draft-related and background variables between UC and NUC players. Because of the matching strategy, there are equal numbers of UC and NUC players during each study year. The number of drafted players ranges from a low of thirty-four in each group in 2011 to fifty-seven per group in 2014. More UC players were drafted in the first round (n = 81) than the number drafted in this round in the NUC group (n = 69). However, there are more second- and third-round draft picks in the NUC group (n = 102, total) compared to the UC group (n = 86, total). The number of players drafted in the fourth round or later is similar in the two groups (n = 58 and 54, respective totals). The mean draft pick number is 64.9 among underclassmen and 66.5 in nonunderclassmen. The median draft selection is fifty-one and fifty-two in the two groups, respectively.

As expected, UCs are about a year younger than NUC players, averaging 21.6 and 22.8 years, respectively. This difference in means is significant. There are also significant between-group differences with respect to weight and position. UC players average about 242 pounds, compared to 253 pounds for NUC players. Player position varies a good deal in the two groups. There are more receivers (28.9 percent) and offensive backs (18.7 percent) in the UC group than in the NUC group, which has 12.9 percent and 12.0 percent of these two position types. NUCs have a higher proportion of offensive linemen (21.3 percent) and defensive backs (39.1 percent) than UCs, who average 8.9 percent and 26.7 percent for these two positions.

Table 5-2 shows that there was a total of fifty arrests in the two groups combined during the five-year study period. However, these arrests were not distributed evenly in the two groups. Thirty-three of the arrests occurred in twenty-four underclassmen, and the remaining seventeen arrests involved thirteen nonunderclassmen. The significance test based on the number of arrests in each group is statistically significant. It can be derived from this information that the thirty-three arrests in the UC group is significantly higher than the seventeen that occurred among NUC players. A total of 10.7 percent of all underclassmen have one or more arrests, compared to 5.8 percent of the nonunderclassmen. The other statistical test for matched pairs fails to reach significance. There are a total of ten players with more than one arrest—six in the UC group and four in the NUC group. Hence, one of four underclassmen with any arrests has multiple arrests. Two players, both underclassmen, have three and four arrests, respectively. The players' age at time of arrest averages twenty-three years in the UC group and twenty-four years in the NUC group, which is a significant difference.

The most common reason for arrest is drugs (*n* = 9), with six players in the UC group and three in NUC being charged with a related crime. This is followed by driving under the influence (DUI), with six in the UC group and two in the NUC group having this charge. Domestic-violence arrests are also higher in the UC group of players, with four arrests, which is double the number in the NUC group. In all, there are seventeen different arrest types or categories that are empirically derived from the data. Underclassmen have more arrests than nonunderclassmen on twelve of these seventeen arrest types, and there is one tie.

DISCUSSION

In 2010, the large majority of college underclassmen who declared for the NFL draft (85 percent) were drafted and played in the NFL. As their numbers nearly doubled, from fifty-three in 2010 to ninety-eight in 2014, a larger number of declared underclassmen played in the NFL, peaking at fifty-seven players in 2014. However, a larger proportion of these declared underclassmen, more than 41 percent in 2014, never got drafted. All underclassmen players who declare for the NFL draft, by rule, lose any remaining eligibility to play college football again. According to the National Collegiate Athletic Association (NCAA) (n.d.), "A current student-athlete loses amateur status in a particular sport by asking to be placed on the draft list or supplemental draft list of a professional league in that sport. Amateur status is lost even if the athlete's name is withdrawn from the draft list before the actual draft, the athlete is not drafted, or the athlete is drafted but does not sign an agreement with a professional team."

Among the 225 underclassmen who did get drafted and played in the NFL between 2010 and 2014, a total of 24, or 10.6 percent, were arrested at least once. This is nearly double the percentage of arrests (5.8 percent) of a sample of nonunderclassmen matched to underclassmen on the basis of draft year and placement (i.e., pick number) in the draft. This matching strategy is successful in creating two groups of players who are drafted in the same year and at a similar place in the draft. There are, however, significant differences between the UC and NUC groups on age (that was expected), position, and weight. It seems unlikely that player position or weight could have a *direct* impact on the incidence of arrests, but this requires further investigation. To the extent that player position and race are related, the relationships between number of arrests and underclassmen versus nonunderclassmen could be affected. This is a potential limitation of this study. However, it was virtually impossible to add position and/or weight as another matching variable.

Age, even just a difference of one year, could play a role in terms of maturity level and potential issues off the playing field. This may be especially relevant for individuals in their early twenties. For example, national-level general-population data for the year 2012 show rapid drops in the number of arrests among males between the ages of twenty and twenty-four. The categories of these arrests include many of the same arrest types as the ones reported for NFL players in this chapter.

There were more than 301,000 arrests in twenty-year-old males (FBI 2012). The number of arrests drops by about fifteen to twenty-five thousand each year for males between the ages of twenty and twenty-four. By age twenty-four, there are less than 247,000 such arrests (FBI 2012). These statistics illustrate a clear decline in arrests among males in the US general population for each year as they proceed through their early twenties. The underclassmen in this study are about a year younger than nonunderclassmen, both at the time they began playing their NFL careers (21.6 versus 22.8 years, respectively) and at the time they were arrested (23.0 and 24.0 years, respectively).

In all, players in the UC group were arrested thirty-three times during the study period, compared to seventeen times in the NUC group. Based on these numbers of arrests, the difference between the UC and NUC groups is significant. However, the other matched-pairs test is not significant. The relationship between UCs/NUCs and arrests, whether statistically significant or not significant, seems consistent and meaningful because more arrests are observed in UC players in twelve of seventeen arrest categories. UC players had two to three times the number of NUC arrests on the three most common arrest types, including drugs, DUI, and domestic violence. The number of arrests is higher for NUC players for only four of seventeen arrest types (plus one tie), and for three of these arrest types, the total number of arrests in the entire sample is only one. All of these results are based on small numbers. Nevertheless, they paint a consistent picture of more arrests among underclassmen versus matched nonunderclassmen controls.

Additional research is required to determine whether the results reported in this chapter can be replicated with larger samples of players. The numbers of players and arrests available for study in this chapter is small, despite the availability of five years of data. As additional years of data become available, it could become easier to uncover significant differences if they do really exist. Nevertheless, it may not be too early for the NFL to recognize underclassmen as a "high-risk" group for arrests and to develop educational, support, and intervention programs that could help minimize the potential for problems. Any player who is arrested once may be at especially high risk of being arrested again, so these players may warrant extra attention.

In several arrest types, professional and college athletes are less likely to be convicted of a serious crime than members of the general population (Waldron 2013). A 2010 Harvard Law School journal article declares, "Conviction rates for athletes are astonishingly low compared to arrest statistics" (Withers 2010). A leading researcher in this area explained this phenomenon as follows: "The athlete's social environment provides him with both protection and support. Accused athletes have money, powerful lawyers, public relations specialists, high-profile coaches, and other popular personalities to come to their defense" (Benedict 2003).

There is also some evidence at the college level that many cases of sexual assault involving student athletes never make it to a courtroom and may be settled behind the closed doors of university-affiliated judicial boards (Benedict 2003).

CONCLUDING REMARKS

Recently, the NFL adopted new policies related to predraft feedback and the evaluation of underclassmen. Each college team can have a maximum of five players evaluated, and college coaches are expected to assist in the guidance of underclassmen with respect to declaring for the NFL draft. The other shift in policy reduces the number of grades or categories (from five to three) that interested underclassmen receive from the NFL Draft Advisory Board. The board uses three categories to classify potential draftees: first-round talent, second-round talent, or "none." It completely dropped the old category "as high as the third round" because it had a history of being inaccurate and was leading underclassmen to make incorrect decisions about their ability to make the NFL. This new system most likely played a role in reducing the number of 2015 underclassmen to seventy-four players, down from the record high of ninety-eight in 2014. The players now declaring for the draft, with the improved guidance and evaluation they are receiving, may, however, be more likely to get drafted. If so, these new policies could continue the trend of an increasing number of underclassmen who play in the league.

REFERENCES

Benedict, J. 2003. "Athletes and Accusations." *NY Times*, August 5. http://www.nytimes.com/2003/08/05/opinion/athletes-and-accusations.html.

Benedict, J., and A. Klein. 1997. "Arrest and Conviction Rates for Athletes Accused of Sexual Assault." *Sociology of Sports Journal* 14 (1): 86–93.

FBI Uniform Crime Reports, Crime in the United States. 2012. "Arrests by Age, 2012." Table 38. http://www.fbi.gov/about-us/cjis/ucr/crime-in-the-u.s/2012/crime-in-the-u.s.-2012/tables/38tabledatadecovervie wpdf.

National Collegiate Athletic Association. n.d. "Remaining Eligible: Professional Draft Inquiries." NCAA. http://www.ncaa.org/remaining-eligible-professional-draft-inquiries.

USA Today. 2010-14. "NFL Player Arrests." http://www.usatoday.com/sports/nfl/arrests/.

Waldron, T. 2013. "Does the NFL Have a Crime Problem? It's Complicated." ThinkProgress. http://thinkprogress.org/sports/2013/06/27/2228241/nfl-complicated-crime-problem/.

Withers, B. P. 2010. "The Integrity of the Game: Professional Athletes and Domestic Violence." *Journal of Sports & Entertainment Law* 1 (1).

	Underclassmen (UC)	Nonunderclassmen Controls (NUC)	p-value
Table 5-1. Background and Draft-Related Variables for Underclassmen and Nonunderclassmen Controls, 2010–14 Seasons Combined			
	(n = 225)	(n = 225)	
Year Drafted	N / %	N / %	
2010	45 / 20.0%	45 / 20.0%	
2011	34 / 15.1%	34 / 15.1%	
2012	41 / 18.2%	41 / 18.2%	1.00
2013	48 / 21.3%	48 / 21.3%	
2014	57 / 25.3%	57 / 25.3%	
Draft Round Selected			
First	81 / 36.0%	69 / 30.7%	
Second	54 / 24.0%	62 / 27.6%	
Third	32 / 14.2%	40 / 17.8%	
Fourth	31 / 13.8%	26 / 11.6%	0.8049
Fifth	14 / 6.2%	16 / 7.1%	
Sixth	9 / 4.0%	8 / 3.6%	
Seventh	4 / 1.8%	4 / 1.8%	
Mean Draft Pick	64.9	66.5	0.7582
Mean Age (in years)	21.6	22.8	< 0.0001
Mean Height (in inches)	73.7	74.2	0.0772
Mean Weight (in pounds)	242.1	253	0.0118
Six-Group Position	N / %	N / %	
Offensive back	42 / 18.7%	27 / 12.0%	
Offensive line	20 / 8.9%	48 / 21.3%	
Receiver	65 / 28.9%	29 / 12.9%	< 0.0001
Defensive back	60 / 26.7%	88 / 39.1%	
Defensive line	38 / 16.9%	33 / 14.7%	

Table 5-2. Number and Type of Arrests among NFL Underclassmen and Nonunderclassmen Matched Controls, 2010–14

Type Arrest	Underclassmen (UC)	Nonunderclassmen Controls (NUC)
Assault	2	1
Battery	0	1
Burglary/Theft	1	0
DUI	6	2
Disorderly conduct	3	1
Domestic violence	4	2
Drugs	6	3
False Name	1	0
Failure to appear	0	1
Gun/Weapon	3	1
License	1	2
Murder	1	0
Outstanding warrant	1	1
Public intoxication	2	1
Reckless driving	1	0
Reckless endangerment	1	0
Resisting arrest	0	1
Total number of arrests	33	17
Total number of players arrested	24	13

Sign/Binomial test (based on number of arrests) p = 0.0328

McNemar's test for matched pairs (p = 0.10)

Part Two
Suspensions and Fines

• • •

CHAPTER 6

Suspensions

• • •

SUSPENSIONS ARE ALMOST CERTAINLY THE most severe punishments meted out to NFL players by the league. In general, suspensions result in missed games and are considerably costlier to players than fines. For some players, particularly marginal ones, a suspension could be the difference between making or remaining on an NFL roster and being cut (Wesseling 2015). The monetary costs of suspensions for players are keyed to the number of games banned and their salaries. Because NFL players earn an average of $1.9 million per year, and most veteran players average about $4 million per year, a suspension of even one game can cost a player thousands and even tens of thousands of dollars. Virtually all *fines* (see chapter 7) are levied for actions that occur on the playing field. In contrast, the large majority of suspensions are a consequence of behaviors that take place off the field.

Roger Goodell took over as commissioner of the NFL on September 1, 2006. Around that time, numerous arrests among NFL players were occurring. In April 2007, the league implemented a new Personal Conduct Policy. This policy imposed quicker and harsher penalties (i.e., suspensions) for players who got in trouble with the law. Based on this new policy, one very promising NFL player was banned from playing in the NFL for the entire 2007 season following five arrests during his brief two-year tenure in the league. A second player who had been arrested four times in fourteen months was suspended for half of the 2007 regular season (Yahoo Sports 2007). Commissioner Goodell wrote to both players, "This is your last opportunity to salvage your NFL career" (Yahoo Sports, Roger Goodell 2007). Interestingly, neither of these players had been convicted for any of their nine arrests at the time their suspensions were given out. The Personal Conduct Policy was enabling the league to impose player suspensions for arrests, even in the absence of convictions. Moreover, because the policy is not a part of the Collective Bargaining Agreement (CBA), the league has additional leeway in handing out suspensions (AP 2014). The 2011 CBA also permits teams to suspend players on their own for conduct detrimental to the team (Tomasson 2011).

In addition to arrests and convictions, suspensions can be given out for offenses like violation of substance abuse policy and use of performance-enhancing drugs (PEDs). Severe on-field violations may also be subject to suspension by the league. In their strictest form, suspensions can be given out for indefinite periods of time and can even result in a player being permanently banned from the league.

Since the time the Personal Conduct Policy started allowing player suspensions for off-field behaviors, there has been a fair amount of controversy related to the length of these bans as well as their consistency. There was a national uproar over the initial two-game suspension given to an NFL player for a domestic-violence incident in the Atlantic City hotel. After Commissioner Goodell admitted publicly that the league had made a mistake by suspending this player for only two games, the NFL policy on domestic violence and suspensions was overhauled. The changes included an automatic six-game suspension for a first-time domestic violence offense and a lifetime banishment from the league for a second (AP 2014). In addition, the two-game ban initially given to the player in question was extended indefinitely (Rosenthal 2014).

Financial loss to suspended players often has implications above and beyond the forfeiture of pay for a specific number of games. Under the 2011 CBA, as well as the specific language included in many players' contracts, suspended individuals may also lose significant percentages of their signing and/or roster bonuses (Florio 2011). In addition to lost pay related to game suspensions, players are also sometimes fined additional "game checks." For example, one player suspended for two games in 2011 was also fined pay for two additional games. Hence, the size of the lost pay was equivalent to four games, and the suspended player forfeited $1.4 million of his $6 million base pay (Craig 2011).

In brief, suspensions can have a significant impact on players and their teams. Promising careers can be affected in critical ways. This chapter addresses the incidence of suspensions in the NFL for a five-year study period. I examine the costs and risk factors for suspensions and analyze the impact of suspensions on game weeks missed by players.

Methods

I used the Spotrac "NFL Fines and Suspensions" database (Spotrac 2015b) as the primary data source for this study. I evaluated all suspensions that occurred during the period January 1, 2010, through December 31, 2014, for inclusion in this study. This makes it possible to analyze each of these five years, from 2010 to 2014, separately or combined. I dropped suspensions that were given to players who never played in at least one NFL regular season. I also excluded suspensions given to players that were retracted or rescinded.

I present numerator-only data for suspensions and did not calculate the rates. The frequency distributions and other statistics adequately document the scope and breadth of NFL suspensions. I give the total number of suspensions by type for each study year and for all years combined. I provide the mean, median, and sum of games suspended by suspension type for the five study years combined. I statistically tested the temporal differences in the number of suspensions. I broke down the total number of suspensions for the entire five-year study period by age group, three-group position (offense, defense, and kicking), six-group position (described in previous chapters), conference (AFC vs. NFC), birthplace region, and NFL team.

I calculated the mean, median, and summed monetary amounts that players forfeited due to suspensions for each type of suspension for all the study years combined. I tested differences for the proportion of suspensions given to offensive versus defensive players, AFC versus NFC players, and team for the five-year study period combined. For the other potential risk-factor variables, I provided numeric comparisons (only) for all regular-season players during the five-year study period.

I analyzed the game weeks impacted by NFL suspensions during the study period. Game weeks are aggregated into quartiles: games one through four, games five through eight, games nine through twelve, and games thirteen through sixteen. I provided the number of player games missed for each of these quartiles for the five study years combined.

RESULTS

During the five-year study period, there was a total of 196 suspensions. I dropped twenty-five of these from the analyses, including sixteen suspended players who never played in a regular-season NFL game, five players who were fined in 2010 but did not play in the NFL after 2009, and four players who had their suspensions completely rescinded. This leaves a total of 171 suspensions for the analyses. Twenty-two of these suspensions involve individuals who played in at least one NFL game in the regular season but did not make an NFL roster the year they were supposed to serve their suspensions. I included these players among those who had been suspended during the study period. However, I did not count the number of games suspended or the monetary amounts associated with these suspensions for these players.

Table 6-1 shows that there are significant temporal differences on the number/proportion of suspensions across study years, peaking at forty-four in 2012 and getting as low as twenty-two and twenty-five in 2010 and 2011, respectively. Seven of every ten suspensions are for either substance abuse or PEDs. The numbers of suspensions for these two charges are similar ($n = 58$ and 62, respectively) for all five study years combined. PEDs suspensions have declined from a high of twenty-four in 2012 to eleven in 2014. Substance-abuse suspensions, however, more than doubled between 2012 ($n = 8$) and 2013 ($n = 17$) and increased even more in 2014 ($n = 21$).

The mean, median, and summed numbers of games by suspension type for all study years combined are shown in table 6-2. (I dropped from this analysis the twenty-two suspended players who did not make an NFL roster during the year the suspension was to be served.) Substance-abuse suspensions have the highest mean number of games suspended, averaging 5.7. This is followed by a mean of 5.6 games per suspension for arrests or convictions. On-field violations have the lowest mean, with 1.2 games suspended, and Personal Conduct Policy suspensions average 1.4 games. Substance abuse has the highest number of summed games suspended with 307, followed by PEDs with 242. Combined, substance abuse and PEDs account for about 80 percent of all games suspended during the five-year study period.

The mean, median, and summed dollar amounts forfeited by type of suspension for all study years combined are also shown in table 6-2. (I also excluded the twenty-two suspended players dropped in the previous paragraph for this analysis. In addition, the Spotrac database does not list the monetary amounts for about 10 percent of all suspensions. These are considered missing and were not counted as part of the statistics.) Mean salary loss per suspension is highest for arrests and convictions ($532,800), substance abuse ($496,900) and conduct detrimental to the team/league ($489,500). There were only two suspensions for undisclosed violations, which have the lowest mean salary amount forfeited. The next-lowest mean amounts per suspension are for on-field violations ($148,500) and Personal Conduct Policy violations ($178,300). Mean monetary suspension amounts average $306,700 for PEDs violations. In general, mean suspension dollar amounts forfeited exceed their respective medians for all suspensions except for the small number of undisclosed suspensions. This indicates that the means are being driven up by one or more very costly suspensions. Because of missing data, the summed monetary amounts for suspensions are not reflective of the actual total dollar value that was forfeited. Nevertheless, substance-abuse suspensions easily have the highest summed amount of forfeited salary, totaling $24.8 million. The next-highest summed suspension type is for PEDs, at $16.6 million.

As shown in table 6-3, more suspensions involve defensive players than offensive players (n = 99 and 69 suspensions, respectively). Excluding kickers, the difference in the proportion of suspensions given to defensive versus offensive players is statistically significant. Age is not related to suspensions, although the youngest age group tends to have a slightly higher proportion of suspensions (41.5 percent) relative to their percentage in the underlying population of regular season players (37.2 percent).

Table 6-4 shows that the team a player is affiliated with is not a significant risk factor for suspensions for the combined five-year period, although this could be due to the relatively small numbers of suspensions per team.

There is, however, a lot of variability among teams in the number of suspensions. For example, the Redskins have thirteen suspensions, followed by the Colts with ten and the Ravens and Seahawks with nine each. The Bills, Eagles, and Raiders have the fewest number of suspensions, with two each.

A total of 150 players received all 171 suspensions included in this analysis. There are eighteen players (12 percent) with more than one suspension during the five-year study period. Nearly half of all suspensions sideline players between weeks one and four of the game. No other game week quartile exceeds 20 percent of the suspension weeks.

DISCUSSION

The total number of NFL suspensions has increased significantly during recent years. Suspensions peaked in 2012 but did not fall back to 2010–11 levels during the next two years. The high number of suspensions in 2012 is, in part, attributable to a large increase in the number of PEDs suspensions. These rise from six and seven in 2010 and 2011, respectively, to twenty-four in 2012. PEDs suspensions drop to fourteen and eleven during 2013 and 2014 but remain the second-most-common suspension type during these two years, behind substance abuse. The number of substance-abuse suspensions doubles during 2013–14 combined with a mean of 19.5 per year versus the previous three, years when the mean is under 7 per year. Since 2012, the combined number of suspensions for substance abuse and PEDs has accounted for 72 percent to 82 percent of all NFL suspensions. During the five-year study period, PEDs and substance abuse represent the charges for nearly 80 percent of the games suspended and 77 percent of forfeited pay.

While PEDs and substance abuse collectively account for a large proportion of all suspensions, they are dissimilar infractions, and the profile of players who are involved in these two types of offenses are different in several respects. For example, about 63 percent of substance-abuse offenders were born in a state in the Southern part of the United States, compared to less than 42 percent of those with PEDs suspensions. About 29 percent of players suspended for PEDs were born in the Western part of the United States, compared to 16 percent of substance-abuse offenders. About 29 percent of PEDs violators are in the oldest age group (twenty-eight years and older), compared to 19 percent of players suspended for substance abuse. Players suspended for PEDs are also more likely to be defensive players (61.3 percent) than are substance-abuse violators, 51.7 percent of whom are defensive players. All of the results described in this paragraph are post hoc and have not been tested statistically.

Athletes may use PEDs to help improve their performance, increase muscle size, and possibly reduce body fat (National Institute of Drug Abuse 2015). Overall, offensive linemen have double the number of PEDs suspensions ($n = 10$) than they do for substance abuse ($n = 4$). More than half of all suspensions committed by offensive linemen during the five-year study period were for PEDs. Surveys indicate that steroid abuse among athletes is at about 6 percent (National Institute of Drug Abuse 2015). Even at its peak in 2012, when there were twenty-four PEDs suspensions, the percentage of NFL players suspended for using PEDs was in the 1 percent range. The apparent decline in PEDs suspensions since 2012 seems encouraging. Still, much more needs to be done with respect to PEDs to reduce its incidence in the NFL. The length of PEDs suspensions during the past five years has been remarkably consistent. More than 87 percent of PEDs suspensions are exactly four games in length. Several longer suspensions, for up to eight games, involve second-time offenders, which is consistent with NFL policies. This type of consistency is not generally the case for most other kinds of suspensions.

Violations of the league's Personal Conduct Policy reflect a broad range of actions that may be subject to suspension. According to one Internet author, "This catchall category [personal conduct violations] includes everything from murder to unsanctioned in-game violence to embarrassing the league on social media" (McCann 2014). Because of the heterogeneity of offenses that are subject to suspension, it becomes difficult to make the punishments consistent. In fact, the consistency with which suspensions for violations of the policy are applied is generally an issue for players (Clayton, ESPN 2014), which has been recognized by NFL officials. Troy Vincent, the executive vice president of NFL football operations, in an interview with ESPN, said the following: "They [the players] raise the question of consistency, and we haven't been...We have to acknowledge that, and we've continued to acknowledge that... As a player, you want consistency...You don't want it all over the board" (ESPN 2014).

In December 2014, the NFL implemented a new Personal Conduct Policy that focuses on arrests for violent crimes. This new policy followed the uproar over the initial two-game suspension for the NFL player who was caught on video assaulting his fiancé. Carried out by a special counsel, the new policy uses independent investigations to make decisions about initial discipline. Paid leave for arrestees during the time of the investigation is another element of the new policy. Finally, the commissioner will continue to play a role during appeals but may also ask an independent panel to resolve the appeal (ESPN 2014). Ongoing empirical evaluation and monitoring of new NFL policies is required to determine their effectiveness in reducing behaviors that result in suspensions.

Even though attempting to improve suspension policies related to violent crimes committed off of the playing field is clearly important and much needed, there was a total of only thirteen suspensions in five years for arrests and convictions, and another nine for violations of the Personal Conduct Policy. Combined, these two types of infractions represent less than 13 percent of all suspensions. Moreover, neither of these suspension types has increased during the five study years. Substance abuse policies especially warrant special attention since this problem appears to be on the rise in the NFL, with the number of suspensions more than doubling during 2013/2014 relative to the prior three years (See table 6-1). Moreover, substance abuse policies, including suspension length, remain uneven and inconsistent.

Nearly 13 percent of all suspensions involve players who fail to make an NFL roster during the year they are supposed to serve their suspensions. While data are not available to test this possibility, this may be a consequence of being suspended, especially for free agents and other marginal players. Obviously, suspended players will be lost for at least one game, and on average, they could miss four or more games. The impact of missed (suspension) games on team outcomes has not been studied. How players perform following a suspension is another interesting question that hasn't been looked at. Team officials may also fear that suspended players will become recidivist offenders, assuming they have an elevated risk of being suspended again in the future, missing more games, and again disrupting their respective teams.

Players suspended for actions on the field commit offenses that are quite serious and dangerous in the eyes of the league. Several players have reputations as being "headhunters" (Rosenthal 2014) for their hits against defenseless opponents, late hits, and illegal hits to the head. The league may not view the fine amounts for these offenses as large enough given the danger they pose—hence the need for suspensions. Clearly, the monetary losses to players for suspensions are greater than those for physical fines (see chapter 7). Nevertheless, it remains unclear whether these suspensions are really large enough to affect change among players earning millions of dollars each year.

The nature of physical fines, many involving illegal hits by the players, creates a situation in which defensive players are more likely to be the ones committing these infractions. This prompted one Internet author to proclaim that fines in the NFL were biased against defensive players, "both in rule and implementation" (Kruse 2013). With the exception of on-field infractions, however, other suspension types like PEDs, substance abuse, and violations of the Personal Conduct Policy have nothing to do with whether one plays an offensive or a defensive position. The elevated incidence of suspensions among defensive players documented in this book is an important finding that requires the attention of NFL officials. Additional research is required to help improve our understanding of the root causes of suspensions in the hope of reducing their incidence, including those committed by defensive players.

Appealing a suspension within the league and/or fighting it in the courts can result in more losses for players. One player appealed a two-game suspension meted out in 2008 plus an additional fine of two game checks. The case went through the court system, and in 2011, a state Supreme Court ruled in favor of the NFL. The player's base pay in 2011 was $6 million, which was $5 million more than his base pay in 2008. The player would have forfeited about $235,000 if he served the suspension in 2008. By 2011, he lost $1.4 million (Craig 2011). Legal fees for players who fight their suspensions in court can also be quite costly. One NFL player spent nearly $1 million in legal fees in his court battle over a suspension (Belson 2011). Unfortunately for this player, he also lost his case.

About half of all suspensions sidelined players during the first four games of the regular season. By chance alone, only about 25 percent of the suspension games missed would occur during the first quartile of games. In this study, players missed about 337 games during the first four weeks of the season due to being suspended. The next-highest number of player games missed due to suspension was 133 during the final quartile of the season. Many suspensions are announced during the off-season and take effect at the start of the next season. This helps explain why so many players are suspended during the first four games of the season. This lopsided distribution of the player games missed due to suspensions can result in competitive advantages and disadvantages, depending on the players and teams involved, particularly during the first quarter of the regular season.

The Spotrac database contains a lot of important and useful data that helped make this chapter possible. Nevertheless, some of the suspension-related dollar amounts contained in this database may be underestimates. In addition to base salary forfeited due to suspensions, players may suffer additional losses that may not be included in the Spotrac database. For example, one player suspended for four games in 2011 forfeited more than $1.85 million in game checks, according to the Spotrac database. However, per the CBA and this player's contract, this same player was also subject to additional losses of half a million dollars in signing and roster bonuses (Florio 2011). To the extent that additional suspension-related losses occur, the monetary values included in this chapter may understate the total amounts. There may also be legal fees, which are definitely not included in the published costs of suspensions.

Concluding Remarks

Suspensions are the most severe punishment the league imposes on players who commit serious policy and other violations. PEDs and substance-abuse suspensions are the most common suspension types, with the number of PEDs infractions declining and substance-abuse offenses on the rise. The profiles of players who get PEDs versus substance-abuse suspensions are quite different. Suspensions are far more common among defensive players. While the forfeited pay due to suspensions may seem like a lot of money, in many cases, salaries and bonuses render lost salaries just a small fraction of many players' total remuneration.

REFERENCES

Associated Press, The Dallas Morning News. 2014. "Roger Goodell: NFL to Change Domestic Violence Policy; Ray Rice Suspension Length Was Mistake." August 28. http://www.dallasnews.com/sports/dallas-cowboys/headlines/20140828-roger-goodell-admits-his-ray-rice-call-was-mistake-as-nfl-changes-policy-on-domestic-abuse.ece.

Belson, K. 2011. "Judge Rules for N.F.L. in Supplement Case." *New York Times*, February 8. http://www.nytimes.com/2011/02/09/sports/football/09starcap.html?_r=1.

Clayton, J. 2014. "Owners OK New Conduct Policy" ESPN, December 11. http://espn.go.com/nfl/story/_/id/12009596/memo-roger-goodell-nfl-owners-outlines-conduct-policy-changes.

Craig, M. 2011. "Kevin Williams Gets Two-Game Suspension" *Star Tribune*, September 3. http://www.startribune.com/kevin-williams-gets-two-game-suspension/129129238/.

ESPN. 2014. "Owners OK New Conduct Policy." http://espn.go.com/nfl/story/_/id/12009596/memo-roger-goodell-nfl-owners-outlines-conduct-policy-changes.

Florio, 2011. M. "Trent Williams' Suspension Will Cost Him Plenty of Money." NBC Sports. http://profootballtalk.nbcsports.com/2011/12/07/trent-williams-suspension-will-cost-him-plenty-of-money/.

Goodell, Roger, quoted in Yahoo Sports. 2007. "CB Jones Suspended for 2007 Season, WR Henry Banned 8 Games." https://ca.sports.yahoo.com/nfl/news?slug=playerconduct.

Kruse, Z. 2013. "The Many Inconsistencies in NFL Fines." *Bleacher Report*. http://bleacherreport.com/articles/1507734-the-many-inconsistencies-in-nfl-fines.

McCann, A. 2014. "The NFL's Uneven History of Punishing Domestic Violence." *FiveThirtyEight* Sports, August 28. http://fivethirtyeight.com/features/nfl-domestic-violence-policy-suspensions/.

National Institute of Drug Abuse, Anabolic Steroid Use. 2015. "Why Do People Use Anabolic Steroids?" http://www.drugabuse.gov/publications/research-reports/anabolic-steroid-abuse/why-do-people-abuse-anabolic-steroids.

Rosenthal, G. 2014. "Ray Rice Released by Ravens, Indefinitely Suspended." NFL. http://www.nfl.com/news/story/0ap3000000391538/article/ray-rice-released-by-ravens-indefinitely-suspended.

Rosenthal, G. 2014. "Redskins' Brandon Meriweather Suspended Two Games." NFL. http://www.nfl.com/news/story/0ap3000000383582/article/redskins-brandon-meriweather-suspended-two-games.

Spotrac. 2015a. "NFL Estimated Career Earnings." http://www.spotrac.com/nfl/washington-redskins/players-name/cash-earnings/.

Spotrac. 2015b. "NFL Fines and Suspensions." http://www.spotrac.com/nfl/fines-suspensions/.

Tomasson, C. 2011. "Chris Cook Suspended without Pay." TwinCities.com. http://blogs.twincities.com/vikings/2011/10/26/chris-cook-suspended-without-pay/.

Vincent, T. 2014. "Owners OK New Conduct Policy." ESPN. http://espn.go.com/nfl/story/_/id/12009596/memo-roger-goodell-nfl-owners-outlines-conduct-policy-changes.

Wesseling, C. 2015. "On the Bubble: 23 AFC Players Who Could Be Cut." NFL. http://www.nfl.com/news/story/0ap3000000473902/article/on-the-bubble-23-afc-players-who-could-be-cut.

Table 6-1. Number of Suspensions in the NFL by Type, 2010–14						
Year ═══>	2010	2011	2012	2013	2014	2010–14
Type of Suspension						
Arrest or conviction	3	1	5	0	4	13
Conduct detrimental to team/league	3	0	4	1	3	11
On-the-field violation	0	2	1	5	2	10
Performance enhancing drugs (PEDs)	6	7	24	14	11	62
Personal conduct policy	4	2	1	1	1	9
Substance abuse	6	6	8	17	21	58
Undisclosed	0	7	1	0	0	8
Total ^	22	25	44	38	42	171

^ The number/percent of suspensions per year was significant based on chi-square test for equal proportions (p = 0.0186).

Table 6-2. Mean, Median, and Summed Dollar Suspension Amounts and Number of Games Suspended in the NFL, 2010–14 Combined

Type of Suspension	S Dollar Amounts				Number of Games Suspended			
	N	Mean	Median	Sum	N	Mean	Median	Sum
Arrest or conviction	9	532,841	223,529	4,795,573	10	5.6	4	56
Conduct detrimental to team/league	10	489,456	124,874	4,894,555	11	4.5	4	49
On-the-field violation	10	148,470	132,941	1,484,703	10	1.2	1	12
Performance enhancing drugs	54	306,663	127,058	16,559,776	59	4.1	4	242
Personal conduct policy	6	178,338	117,059	1,070,027	7	1.4	1	10
Substance abuse	50	496,898	173,044	24,844,917	54	5.7	4	307
Undisclosed	2	109,853	109,853	219,705	3	4	4	16
Total *	141	382,051	149,294	53,869,256	154	4.5	4	688

*22 suspended players who played in 1+ NFL regular season, but failed to make an NFL roster during the year that they were supposed to serve their suspensions, were dropped from this analysis. Additional missing data as well.

Table 6-3. Potential Risk Factors for Suspensions in the NFL, 2010–14 Combined				
	Players with Suspensions		All Regular Season NFL Players	
	N	%	N	%
Age Group				
24 years and under	71	41.5%	3,574	37.2%
25 - 27 years	52	30.4%	3,161	32.9%
28+ years	48	28.1%	2,886	30.0%
Position				
*Three-Group^*				
Offense	69	40.3%	4,543	47.2%
Defense	99	57.9%	4,710	49.0%
Kicking	3	18.0%	368	3.8%
Six-Group				
Offensive back	19	11.1%	1,231	12.8%
Offensive line	18	10.5%	1,625	16.9%
Receiver	32	18.7%	1,687	17.5%
Defensive back	72	42.1%	3,237	33.7%
Defensive line	27	15.8%	1,473	15.3%
Kicking	3	18.0%	368	38.0%
*Conference ^^*				
AFC	87	50.9%	4,844	50.3%
NFC	84	49.1%	4,777	49.7%
Birthplace Region				
Midwest	28	16.4%	N/A	
Northeast	21	12.2%		
South	85	49.7%		
West	37	21.6%		
Note: Four players born in foreign countries were excluded.				
^ Significant based on chi-square test for equal proportions (p = 0.0206)				
^^Not significant based on chi-square test for equal proportions.				

Table 6-4. Number of Suspensions by NFL Teams, 2010–14 Combined		
NFL Teams	N	%
Redskins	13	7.6
Colts	10	5.9
Ravens	9	5.3
Seahawks	8	4.7
Broncos	8	4.7
Browns	8	4.7
Panthers	6	3.5
Vikings	6	3.5
Bucs	6	3.5
Giants	6	3.5
Patriots	6	3.5
Rams	6	3.5
Titans	6	3.5
Bengals	5	2.9
Steelers	5	2.9
Cardinals	5	2.9
Chiefs	5	2.9
Dolphins	5	2.9
Lions	5	2.9
Texans	5	2.9
Saints	4	2.3
49ers	4	2.3
Falcons	4	2.3
Jaguars	4	2.3
Jets	4	2.3
Bears	3	1.8
Chargers	3	1.8
Cowboys	3	1.8
Packers	3	1.8
Bills	2	1.2
Eagles	2	1.2
Raiders	2	1.2
Total	171	100.0

CHAPTER 7

Physical Fines

● ● ●

THE NFL COLLECTIVE BARGAINING AGREEMENT (CBA) of 2011 laid the groundwork for a system of fines that penalize players for on-field infractions. These fines may be in addition to yardage penalties assessed during the course of a game, or they may arise after league officials review game tapes, even in the absence of yardage penalties (NFL Ops 2015; NFL 2011). These fines are different from suspensions, which are typically related to off-field actions, like the use of PEDs or substance abuse.

Some fines are given for offenses that are not physical in nature, like taunting an opponent or making an obscene gesture. Other fines involve physical contact, sometimes excessive contact. Plays that have serious consequences for opponents, like concussions (AP 2010; Steele 2013; Fainaru-Wada and Baumgartor 2014; Brooks 2011); broken legs (Fainaru-Wada and Baumgartor 2014); tears of body parts (Grossman 2015); and ending another player's season (Caple 2011), can result in fines.

The fine money collected by the league goes to charitable causes. These include retired player programs and disaster-relief and health-related charities (NFL 2010). Fined players receive a formal letter from the league that details the infraction and stipulates where the fine money goes (Krichavsky, quoted in *USA Today* 2010). Charitable organizations that have received NFL fine money include the Brian Piccolo Cancer Fund, the Vincent T. Lombardi Cancer Research Center, the ALS Neuromuscular

Research Foundation, the NFLPA Player Assistance Trust, and the Red Cross (Kruse 2013).

The CBA of 2011 includes structured fine schedules for specific infractions with minimum monetary amounts for both first- and second-time offenders. According to the agreement (NFL CBA 2011), the minimum fine amounts are to be increased by 5 percent per year during the life of the agreement (NFL CBA 2011). Moreover, the CBA states that the league can impose larger monetary fines for infractions that are "flagrant or gratuitous" (NFL CBA 2011). Hence, the published fine schedule is a guideline that the league can modify given the timing and specifics of a situation. Moreover, and according to the CBA, second-time offenders (of the same infraction) can be fined larger amounts, usually double the amount of the first offense.

Several sports writers have documented inconsistencies in the fine system that occurred in the years following the 2011 CBA. According to one critic, more than 30 percent of the fines the NFL levied in 2012 were outside of the published limits (Kruse 2013). Another inconsistency of the fine schedule is that it fails to coincide with current player-safety concerns. According to one Internet author, fines may be biased against defensive players (Kruse 2013).

There is no scientific literature that focuses on the epidemiology of fines in the NFL. There are numerous sports articles on the Internet that attempt to address various aspects of the topic. The existing papers, however, lump together fines that are and are not for physical infractions, and also may include suspensions. This chapter focuses on the incidence, costs, and risk factors of NFL fines that involve physical contact. I examine trends over a five-year study period.

METHODS

I reviewed all fines listed in the Spotrac "NFL Fines and Suspensions" database (2015) between 2010 and 2014. I first separated these fines into those based on infractions of a physical nature and those that were not.

Those based on nonphysical offenses include offenses like taunting, excessive celebrating, throwing a football into the stands, sending personal messages during a game, and uniform/equipment violations. I dropped the fines for nonphysical causes from the analyses in this chapter. The remaining fines, which I refer to as "physical fines," are physical in nature and include late hits, roughing the passer, physical contact with a referee, helmet-to-helmet hits, and fifteen other types of infractions.

Fines for "unsportsmanlike conduct" may or may not be physical in nature. The Spotrac descriptions of fines for unsportsmanlike conduct indicate physical actions like "head butting" or "unnecessary roughness." Obviously, offenses like these must be counted as physical fines. In other instances, however, fines for unsportsmanlike conduct are not physical at all. One player was given an unsportsmanlike-conduct fine after "removing his helmet on the field of play" during a week seventeen game in 2014 (Spotrac 2015). I checked all fines for "unsportsmanlike conduct" against reliable Internet sources to determine whether they were physical or nonphysical. I included the former fines in the analysis and dropped the latter. I included fines that occurred during the pre- or postseasons in the analysis, as long as they involved players who participated in the respective regular seasons.

I did not compute any rates in this chapter because numerators alone and frequency distributions provide a complete picture of the problem. I show a frequency distribution of all eligible physical fines for each of the five study years, 2010 through 2014, plus all of the years combined. I categorize all physical fines that occurred during the regular season based on four- to five-week periods as follows: weeks one through four, weeks five through eight, weeks nine through twelve, and weeks thirteen through seventeen. I displayed the number of physical fines that occurred in each of these periods for each study year and all years combined. I broke down the total number of physical fines for the entire five-year study period by age group, three-group position (offense, defense, and kicking), six-group position (used in previous chapters), conference (AFC vs. NFC), and birthplace region.

I performed a statistical test on the number of fines by study year and combined the number of fines by four- to five-week periods for all five study years. I also tested the differences for the proportion of fines given to offensive versus defensive players, as well as AFC versus NFC players for the five years of the study combined. For some potential risk-factor variables, I displayed (but did not statistically test) league averages for the combined five years of the study period.

Each fine is associated with a monetary amount. I have provided the mean and median fine amount in US dollars by each physical fine type. I also showed the monetary sum of all physical fine types. I created a summary table display that contains the following for each study year and for all years combined: total number of fines; total number of players who were fined; and mean, median, and summed monetary value of the fines.

RESULTS

As shown in table 7-1, there were a total of 726 physical fines during the five-year study period. This averages to 145 physical fines per year. However, there is a significant difference in the number of fines meted out during the five study years. The first two study years, 2010 and 2011, have fewer physical fines (102 and 89) compared to the latter three years. The total number of physical fines peaked in 2012 and 2013 (at 194 and 191) but then declined in 2014 (to 150). The most common types of physical fines for the combined five-year study period are roughing the passer ($n = 158$; 21.8 percent); a late hit ($n = 101$; 13.9 percent); and a hit on a defenseless player ($n = 90$; 12.4 percent). Helmet-to-helmet hits ($n = 56$; 7.7 percent) and fighting ($n = 53$; 7.3 percent) are the only other two physical fine types with frequencies of more than fifty during the five-year study period. Twenty-four unsportsmanlike-conduct fines are physical in nature, with half of these occurring during 2014. About 25 percent of all unsportsmanlike-conduct fines listed in the Spotrac database are nonphysical, and I dropped them from all analyses.

Table 7-2 shows that there is a significant difference in the number of physical fines given out based on the quartile of the regular season. The largest number of physical fines occur during the first four weeks of the regular season (n = 230; 33.3 percent). The next four-week period has the fewest number of physical fines (n = 136; 19.7 percent).

As shown in table 7-3, among all regular-season players during the five-year study period, older players in the age range of twenty-eight and older are slightly overrepresented among individuals receiving physical fines and are underrepresented in the youngest age range. For example, 37 percent of players who received physical fines were twenty-eight years old and older versus 30 percent of all regular-season players during the study period. This pattern is reversed for the youngest age group.

Defensive players, who represent about 49 percent of all regular-season players during the study period, received 74 percent of all physical fines; offensive players received only 25 percent of such fines. The difference in the proportions of physical fines given to offensive versus defensive players is significant. (Kickers were excluded from this analysis.) Analyses of the six-group position variable reveal that defensive backs represented 33.7 percent of all regular-season players but received about half of all physical fines. Similarly, defensive linemen represented 15.3 percent of the total player population but got 24.2 percent of all physical fines. All three offensive groups of players (offensive linemen, offensive backs, and receivers) are underrepresented among those with physical fines relative to their numbers among all regular-season players during the study period. NFC players encompass 55.4 percent of those who were given physical fines versus 44.6 percent of AFC players, and this difference in proportions is significant.

Table 7-4 shows that there is considerable variability in the number of physical fines given out during the five-year study period based on team. These difference in the proportion of physical fines among teams is significant. The Ravens and Lions have the most physical fines of any team (n = 45 and 43, respectively), followed by the Titans and Redskins (n = 38 and 36 respectively). The teams with the fewest number of physical fines are the Chiefs (n = 8), Jaguars, and Chargers (n = 10 each).

The 726 physical fines during the study period were given out to a total of 487 different players. The large majority of players (n = 351; 72.1 percent) had one physical fine, and another eighty-three (17 percent) had two. About 11 percent of players with physical fines received three or more. The player with the most physical fines had eight.

The number of physical fines for all twenty types of fines, along with their monetary mean, median, and sum dollar amounts, are shown in table 7-5. The most common physical fine type is roughing the passer (n = 158), with a mean and median fine amount of $15,200 and $15,750, respectively. A late hit is the second most common fine type (n = 104), with a mean and median fine amount of $9,400 and $7,900, respectively. There are much fewer fines for physical contact with an official (n = 8) and low block (n = 6), but these two fine types have the highest mean fine amounts, both averaging more than $24,500 per fine. However, the mean for a low block is skewed by a single fine of $100,000 that was given out in the 2013 regular season (Hanzus 2013). Helmet-to-helmet hits (n = 56) also have a large mean fine amount, averaging just over $23,000.

The results in table 7-5 are sorted by the fine types, with the highest to lowest summed dollar values for the five-year study period combined. Four fine types encompassed more than $6.4 million of the total $10.5 million meted out for all physical fines during the study period. These four fine types and their summed dollar values are roughing the passer ($2.4 million), a hit on a defenseless player ($1.7 million), a helmet-to-helmet hit (nearly $1.3 million), and a late hit ($978,000).

DISCUSSION

I uncovered two types of temporal trends in this study with respect to the incidence of physical fines. First, there are two years, 2012 and 2013, when the number of physical fines were much higher than for the other three years. During those two years, there was an average of 186.0 physical fines per year. During the other three study years, the average is 106.3 physical fines. This is a nearly 75 percent difference in the mean number of physical fines between these two groups of years. The physical-fine types that had the highest numeric increase during 2012 and 2013 are the same as the three most common types of physical fines for the five-year study period combined: roughing the passer, hits on a defenseless player, and late hits. For example, there is a total of fifty-six fines for hits on defenseless players during 2012 and 2013 combined. During the other three years, there is a total of thirty-four such fines. On a per-year basis, this averages to 28.0 and 11.3 hits on defenseless players in 2012–13 versus the other three study years, respectively. It is impossible to know whether these types of increases reflect a different threshold by the league in giving fines for these types of infractions or whether players are committing these offenses more often. Another intriguing question is whether the increased number of fines in 2012 and 2013 impacted the incidence of injuries, like concussions.

The other significant temporal trend is related to the timing of physical fines during the course of a season. For all five study years combined, one-third of all physical fines were given out during the first four weeks of the regular season. This percentage dropped off to under 20 percent during weeks five through eight and then leveled off during the final nine weeks of the regular season. It is possible that the league attempts to "send a message" to players early in the season. Alternatively, players could be testing the officials to see how much they will tolerate.

Players fined for the same offense more than once are supposed to be given larger fines. According to the published schedule of fines in the 2011 CBA, second-time offenders (of the same infraction) can be fined at double the amount of the first offense (Kruse 2013). It is unclear, however, whether a player will be fined increasing amounts over time if he commits *different* infractions.

One NFL player was fined five times for physical offenses during the study period—twice in 2012 and 2014 and once in 2013. The fine given to this player for fighting in 2012 was $7,875. This is less than the mean and median of all fighting fines during the study period. More importantly, this is $18,600 less than the NFL minimum for fighting as a first offense. (Kruse 2013) This same player was fined twice for late hits, once in 2012 and once in 2013. He was fined twice as much for the first late hit ($15,750) in 2012 as he was for the second one in 2013. In 2014, this same player was fined $8,268 for a helmet-to-helmet hit. The mean and median fines for helmet-to-helmet hits for all study years combined are about $23,000 and $21,000, respectively, and the NFL minimum for a first offense of this kind is $21,000. Despite this being the player's fourth offense during the study period (and it is possible that this player had other fines prior to the start of this study that were not recorded), he was fined considerably less for this offense than the average of other players for the same offense and also far less than the league minimum for a first offense. Finally, this player's fifth physical fine during the study period was for a hit on a defenseless player. This player's fine was $10,000, which is about half of the mean and median fines of all players for this infraction and also about half of the NFL minimum for a first offense of $21,000.

In addition to inconsistencies within physical fine types, there are sometimes issues with the monetary amounts relative to nonphysical fines. As Kruse notes, some fines for "uniform violations" exceed the amounts for "unsportsmanlike conduct" and "face mask" infractions (Kruse 2013). In 2010, for example, one player was fined $2,500 for a late hit. That same year, the same player was fined $5,000 for throwing a football into the stands. Another player was fined $10,500 for a uniform/equipment violation in 2013. In the following year, the same player was fined $8,268 for an unsportsmanlike-conduct infraction that involved head-butting an opponent. Given the many inconsistencies in the NFL's fine system, it should not be surprising that the player, said to be the "most fined in the NFL" (Grossman 2015), did not have a single *physical* fine during the period 2010 through 2014; all of his fines were for nonphysical offenses.

Based on these and many other similar inconsistencies, it cannot be ruled out that the NFL fine system requires rethinking and, possibly, revamping. The selected cases just described (as well as numerous others not presented in this chapter) indicate that inconsistencies may exist, which warrants league and NFLPA attention. The messages being sent to players based on inconsistencies in the fine structure may be confusing. Fines that inflate the significance of relatively trivial infractions, not involving injury to other players, may minimize the importance of much more serious offenses.

While the five-year summed physical fine amounts presented in this chapter may seem like a lot of money (i.e., nearly $10.5 million), this amount needs to be considered in light of the magnitude of some of the actions being committed, as well as their potential impact on opponent-player victims. The salaries that NFL players are paid should be taken into account as well.

It is generally accepted that NFL regular-season players earn an average of about $1.9 million per year (Burke 2012). The mean fine amount per (fined) player, per year, averages about $14,428 during the 2010–14 study period. From these numbers, the percentage of players' salary encompassed by physical fines can be computed. In fact, players with physical fines pay less than 1 percent of their total salaries for these offenses. These estimates are based on statistics for NFL players overall and have not been adapted to each of the actual player offenders documented in this chapter. Given the severity of some of the physical fines being committed by NFL players and their potential for serious injury impacts on opposing players, does it make sense that the mean fine amounts per player are less than 1 percent of players' salaries?

One player, who had one of the highest numbers of physical fines, earned more than $20 million during a three-year period when many of these fines were being committed (AP 2010).

It is a surprise to me that National Football Conference (NFC) players have a significantly higher proportion of physical fines than American Football Conference (AFC) players. The analysis of fines by team reveals that the six teams with the lowest number of physical fines during the entire study are all AFC teams. Moreover, ten of the fourteen teams with the largest numbers of physical fines are NFC teams. The reasons for differences between conferences are unknown. Additional analyses of team data are required to help shed additional light on this finding.

There are very large differences between offensive and defensive players as far as the number and proportion of physical fines meted out. At least one sports writer considers the difference in fine amounts between the two types of players a "bias" (Kruse 2013). Rather than a bias, it may instead be due to the very nature and types of physical fines. Some offenses, like late hits, face-mask hits, and helmet-to-helmet hits, inherently seem like infractions that defensive players are more likely to commit. Moreover, these are some of the most common types of physical fines. Infractions like unsportsmanlike conduct and even hits on defenseless players may be committed by offensive players, but again, they may be more common infractions for defensive players. It is certainly possible that offensive linemen and offensive backs are given physical fines, but their roles on the field generally minimize this as a possibility. Defensive players especially should be targeted with respect to extra education and training to help avoid or minimize their involvement in committing physical infractions and endangering their victims—usually game opponents.

About 28 percent of all physical fines are recidivist in nature. Repeat physical fines, however, may not involve the same offenses by players. Consequently, players committing multiple offenses that are different may not be subject to the larger fine amounts associated with repeat infractions of the same fine type. This policy may require revision in light of the scope of the problem and the potential for physical harm to otherwise-innocent opponent victims. Given the high level of physical-fine recidivism, the current NFL fine schedule does not appear to be a deterrent to committing these infractions. Improving education and training programs directed at reducing the number of physical fines, particularly among repeat offenders, would seem like a high priority for the league and the NFL Players Association. The 5 percent yearly increase in fine amounts required by the 2011 CBA also does not seem to be acting as a deterrent; the number of physical fines was significantly higher in 2012 and 2013, after two increases to the fine schedule had already been implemented.

Concluding Remarks

Dangerous play in the NFL can result in serious injuries for affected players. In an effort to improve sportsmanship and reduce the incidence of injuries due to dangerous play, the NFL has implemented a system of fines. Unfortunately, this system is inconsistent and has not deterred players from committing these infractions. This is evident from the high number of physical fines during a five-year period, as well as the large number of repeat offenders. Relative to players' salaries, fine amounts are not large enough to effect real change. Education and training aimed at minimizing dangerous play resulting in physical fines, especially for defensive players, requires attention and monitoring.

References

AP. 2010. "NFL Fines 3 Players Total of $175k." ESPN.go.com. http://sports.espn.go.com/nfl/news/story?id=5703113.

Brooks, M. 2012. "James Harrison Suspension Upheld by NFL." *Washington Post*, December 16. http://www.washingtonpost.com/blogs/early-lead/post/james-harrison-suspension-upheld-by-nfl/2011/12/16/gIQAYZQUyO_blog.html.

Burke, M. 2012. "Average Player Salaries in the Four Major American Sports Leagues." *Forbes*, December 7. http://www.forbes.com/sites/monteburke/2012/12/07/average-player-salaries-in-the-four-major-american-sports-leagues/.

Caple, C. "Trent Cole Fined $7,500 for Ending Russell Okung's Season." *Seahawks* blog, December 7. http://blog.seattlepi.com/football/2011/12/07/trent-cole-fined-just-7500-for-ending-russell-okungs-season/.

Fainaru-Wada, M., and S. Baumgart. "The NFL's Tackling Dilemma." ESPN. http://espn.go.com/espn/otl/story/_/id/11466663/nfl-players-grudgingly-adjust-new-tackling-rules-avoid-head-injuries.

Grossman, E. 2015. "Why Marshawn Lynch Tops the List of the Most Fined in the NFL." *Men's Journal*. http://www.mensjournal.com/adventure/races-sports/why-marshawn-lynch-tops-the-list-of-the-most-fined-in-the-nfl-20150126.

Hanzus, D. 2013. "Ndamukong Suh Fined $100k by NFL for Illegal Block." NFL. http://www.nfl.com/news/story/0ap1000000242024/article/ndamukong-suh-fined-100k-by-nfl-for-illegal-block.

Krichavsky, D., quoted in *USA Today*. 2010. "Where Does the Fine Money Go?" *USA Today*, October 30. http://usatoday30.usatoday.com/sports/football/nfl/2010-10-29-1108672472_x.htm.

Kruse, Z. 2013. "The Many Inconsistencies in NFL Fines." *Bleacher Report*. http://bleacherreport.com/articles/1507734-the-many-inconsistencies-in-nfl-fines.

Manfred, T. 2013. "Two Charts That Expose How Badly NFL Players Get Paid." *Business Insider*, September 5. http://www.businessinsider.com/charts-expose-how-badly-nfl-players-get-paid-2013-9.

NFL. 2010. "Where Does On-Field Fine Money Go?" NFL Communications. http://nflcommunications.com/2010/12/22/where-does-on-field-fine-money-go/.

———. 2011a. "League Discipline." https://nfllabor.files.wordpress.com/2011/09/2011-league-discipline.pdf.

————. 2011b. "NFL Collective Bargaining Agreement." Article 46, Section 1d, https://nfllabor.files.wordpress.com/2010/01/collective-bargaining-agreement-2011-2020.pdf.

NFL Ops. 2015. "Fines and Appeals: The NFL's Schedule of Infractions and Fines, and a Process for Appeal." http://operations.nfl.com/football-ops/fines-appeals/.

Spotrac. 2015. "NFL Fines and Suspensions." http://www.spotrac.com/nfl/fines-suspensions/.

Steele, D. 2013. "NFL Doesn't Hit Where It Hurts—Choosing Fines over Suspensions." *Sporting News*, September 26. http://www.sportingnews.com/nfl/story/2013-09-25/nfl-fines-suspensions-ndamukong-suh-dashon-goldson-repeat-offenders-cba.

Table 7-1. Frequency of Physical Fines in the NFL, 2010–14							
Year ===>	2010	2011	2012	2013	2014	2010-14	
Type of Physical Fine	N	N	N	N	N	N	%
Blindside block	0	2	6	4	7	19	2.6%
Chop block	4	2	3	1	2	12	1.7%
Clipping	0	0	2	2	0	4	0.6%
Crown-of-helmet violation	0	0	0	4	0	4	0.6%
Face mask	10	3	19	23	19	74	10.2%
Fighting	10	7	13	6	17	53	7.3%
Helmet-to-helmet hit	12	7	17	14	6	56	7.7%
Hit on defenseless player	17	9	30	26	8	90	12.4%
Horse-collar-tackle	4	7	17	8	8	44	6.1%
Impermissible use of helmet	0	1	0	0	0	1	0.1%
Late hit	18	13	28	25	20	101	13.9%
Leg whip	1	1	1	3	2	8	1.1%
Low block	0	3	2	1	0	6	0.8%
Peelback block	0	0	1	2	0	3	0.4%
Physical contact with official	0	1	1	4	2	8	1.1%
Roughing the passer	20	26	33	47	32	158	21.8%
Spearing	5	0	0	1	0	6	0.8%
Striking/Kicking/Kneeing	1	6	16	13	11	47	6.5%
Entering fight area	0	0	0	1	4	5	0.7%
Unsportsmanlike conduct	0	1	5	6	12	24	3.3%
Totals	102	89	194	191	150	726	100%

Table 7-2. Week of Season of Physical Fines in the NFL, 2010–14							
Year ===>	2010	2011	2012	2013	2014	2010-14	
Week of Season	N	N	N	N	N	N	%
1 through 4	28	49	59	62	32	230	33.3%
5 through 8	23	14	28	41	30	136	19.7%
9 through 12	17	17	65	32	30	161	23.3%
13 through 17	26	5	40	45	48	164	23.7%
Totals ^	94	85	192	180	140	691	100%

Note: 23 Physical fines during the preseason and 10 from the postseason were dropped from analysis.

^ Year and week of season were significant based on chi-square test for equal proportions ($p < 0.0001$)

Table 7-3. Potential Risk Factors for Physical Fines in the NFL, 2010–14 Combined				
	Players with Physical Fines		All NFL Players	
	N	%	N	%
Age Group (in years)				
24 and under	227	31.3%	3,574	37.2%
25 - 27	228	31.4%	3,161	32.9%
28+	271	37.3%	2,886	30.0%
Position				
*3-Group^*				
Offense	182	25.1%	4,543	47.2%
Defense	538	74.1%	4,710	49.0%
Kicking	6	8.0%	368	3.8%
6-Group				
Offensive back	31	4.3%	1,231	12.8%
Offensive line	86	11.8%	1,625	16.9%
Receiver	65	9.0%	1,687	17.5%
Defensive back	362	49.9%	3,237	33.7%
Defensive line	176	24.2%	1,473	15.3%
Kicking	6	0.8%	368	380.0%
*Conference ^^*				
AFC	324	44.6%	4,844	50.3%
NFC	402	55.4%	4,777	49.7%
Birthplace Region				
Midwest	115	16.6%	NA	
Northeast	69	9.9%		
South	375	54.0%		
West	135	19.5%		

^ Significant based on chi-square test for equal proportions (p < 0.0001)
(Kickers were excluded)
^^ Significant based on chi-square test for equal proportions (p < 0.0038)

Table 7-4. Number of Physical Fines by NFL Teams, 2010–14 Combined		
NFL Teams	N	%
Ravens	45	6.2%
Lions	43	5.9%
Titans	38	5.2%
Redskins	36	5.0%
Patriots	32	4.4%
Rams	32	4.4%
Giants	31	4.3%
Vikings	29	4.0%
Eagles	27	3.7%
Steelers	27	3.7%
Packers	26	3.6%
Panthers	26	3.6%
Bears	25	3.4%
49ers	24	3.3%
Jets	23	3.2%
Cardinals	22	3.0%
Texans	22	3.0%
Broncos	18	2.5%
Falcons	18	2.5%
Raiders	18	2.5%
Bills	17	2.3%
Bucs	16	2.2%
Cowboys	16	2.2%
Seahawks	16	2.2%
Colts	15	2.1%
Saints	15	2.1%
Browns	14	1.9%
Dolphins	14	1.9%
Bengals	13	1.8%
Chargers	10	1.4%
Jaguars	10	1.4%
Chiefs	8	1.1%
Total	726	100%
The difference among teams was significant (p<0.001)		

Table 7-5. Mean, Median, and Summed Physical Fine Amounts in the NFL, 2010–14 Combined				
	$ Dollar Amounts 2010–14 Combined			
Type of Physical Fine	N	Mean	Median	Sum
Roughing the passer	158	15,208	15,750	2,402,862
Hit on defenseless player	90	19,224	20,000	1,730,119
Helmet-to-helmet hit	56	23,058	21,000	1,291,255
Late hit	104	9,403	7,875	977,896
Striking/Kicking/Kneeing	47	24,337	8,268	688,644
Fighting	53	12,372	8,268	655,698
Horse collar tackle	44	14,280	15,750	628,287
Face mask	74	8,138	7,875	602,216
Blindside block	19	20,755	21,000	394,350
Unsportsmanlike conduct	24	10,116	8,268	242,787
Physical contact with official	8	24,574	26,250	196,589
Low block	6	24,646	8,938	147,875
Spearing	6	17,667	12,500	106,000
Leg whip	8	12,757	12,009	102,055
Chop block	12	7,065	7,688	84,786
Crown-of-helmet violation	4	19,688	21,000	78,750
Clipping	4	12,875	12,875	51,500
Entering fight area	5	8,614	8,268	43,072
Peelback block	3	10,000	10,000	30,000
Impermissible use of helmet	1	20,000	20,000	20,000
Totals	726	14,428	10,000	10,474,741

Part Three
Career Chaos

• • •

CHAPTER 8

The End of Playing Careers following Placement on the Injured Reserve List (IRL)

• • •

INJURIES, SPANNING THE SEVERITY SPECTRUM from mild to life-threatening or even fatal, are an inevitable outcome of a violent contact sport like American football. At the high school and college levels, several deaths directly attributable to playing football occur in most years (Mueller and Cantu 2011). However, the NFL, in its current AFL/NFL merged format that began in 1970, has never had a death on the playing field directly attributable to football during a regular-season game (Miller 2013). Nevertheless, the many serious injuries experienced by NFL players each year may have significant playing and career consequences. These include missed games, missed seasons, and even career endings for players.

The most severe injuries result in players being placed on the league's Injured Reserve List (IRL). These could include broken limbs; torn muscles; and neck, back, and spine injuries, as well as injuries that require surgery. Up until the 2012 season, players placed on the IRL, by rule, could not return to play that year. Beginning with the 2012 season, a short-term IRL designation was established, and one player per team was allowed to return to play during the season (Maske 2012).

Despite all of the missed games associated with serious injuries and IRL injuries specifically, the scope of this problem has never been systematically examined or quantified. This chapter documents the incidence of IRL injuries in the NFL during a five-year period, from 2010 to 2014. In addition, I assessed the effect of IRL injuries on NFL career endings for two cohorts of regular-season players. I also examined the impact of specific injury types linked to IRL injuries on career endings.

LITERATURE REVIEW

Although a PubMed search using the term "Injured Reserve List" produced no results, the more general term "NFL injuries" yielded 135 journal articles. Some of these papers deal with the time it takes to return to play following specific types of injuries and the procedures that are used to treat them. For example, Erickson and colleagues (2014) examined "return to sport" rates among NFL quarterbacks who suffered anterior cruciate ligament (ACL) ruptures and underwent reconstructive surgery. Twelve out of thirteen of the quarterbacks were able to return to the league following this procedure and played for an average of nearly five years after returning. Using the NFL's "Sports Injury Monitoring System" surveillance database for 2000 to 2012, Lynch et al. (2013) determined lost playing time among 727 players with shoulder injuries involving the acromioclavicular (AC) joint. On average, affected players missed fewer than ten days. However, players with AC joint injuries that required surgery missed a mean of more than fifty-six days. Hsu and colleagues (2010) conducted a study of outcomes following lumbar disc herniation (LDH) among 342 elite professional athletes in several sports, including football. About 82 percent of all LDH athletes were able to return to their respective sports, with an average career length of 3.4 years. Other studies of NFL players and the time taken to return to play focus on injuries like proximal tendon avulsions of the hamstring (Mansour et al. 2013), isolated tears of the quadriceps tendons treated with surgery (Boublik et al. 2013), and patellar tendon ruptures (Boublik et al. 2011).

Existing studies provide knowledge about specific injuries and the length of time required for NFL players to return to play. However, I could not locate any papers that focus specifically on the Injured Reserve

List or how injuries affect career ending among players. To address this gap, this study follows a large number of NFL players for up to three to four years following IRL placement to determine subsequent levels of career endings in the league.

METHODS

This study aggregates data on every NFL player who played at least one regular-season game between 2010 and 2014. I identified these players using weekly NFL team rosters (NFL, Team Rosters 2010-14) that I collected from information on all five regular seasons from the NFL website. I determined the playing time for each player based on NFL game logs (NFL, Game Logs 2010-14). These logs indicate the seasons played by each player, as well as the specific games played each year. The study cohort of players is dynamic because players could play as few as one and as many as all five of the regular seasons of interest. Within each of these seasons, players could play between one and sixteen regular season games. I studied only the 2010–14 regular seasons and excluded from consideration all pre- and postseason data during those years. The rationale for this exclusion again has to do with denominator calculations and resource considerations.

I obtained IRL data from NFL transaction reports published daily, all year around, on both the NFL and ESPN websites (NFL, Transactions 2010-14; ESPN, NFL Transactions 2010-14). I recorded the types of IRL injuries and included them in the analysis. Types of IRL injuries are generally published online in a one- to two-word description that denotes the affected body part, such as "knee," "shoulder," "hamstring," or "concussion." Players are counted as being on the IRL only if they played one or more regular-season games during one or more study years. I excluded players placed on the IRL during the preseason who never played a regular-season game.

For players in the 2010 and 2011 seasons, I conducted a longitudinal analysis of IRL status and career ending. I classified the players by

IRL and injury status into the following three groups: (1) IRL players, (2) non-IRL players (including those who missed at least three regular-season games immediately following an injury), and (3) all remaining players (i.e., those with no IRL and who did not miss more than three games following an injury). The latter two groups serve as controls for this study. I obtained players' missed games following an injury using NFL injury reports (NFL, Injury Reports 2010-14), in conjunction with the game logs (NFL, Game Logs 2010-14) described in the previous paragraph. On its website, the NFL publishes injury reports weekly during the NFL season for about 89 percent of all games played during the regular season. It does not publish injury reports for the following: (1) the week prior to a team's bye week and (2) following the final week of the regular season for teams not playing in the first round of the playoffs. Therefore, 28 of the 256 regular season games (11 percent) are not covered by the NFL Injury Report. In the "Discussion" section, I explain the implications of these missing injury reports with respect to this study.

I compared the career endings of three player groups, assessing them by the relevant number of subsequent seasons missed. Specifically, I categorized 2010 players who did not play in any of the next four regular seasons (2011 through 2014) as "career-ended." Similarly, I considered 2011 NFL players who did not play in any of the next three regular seasons (2012 through 2014) as "career-ended." The assumptions regarding career ending after three to four seasons reflects patterns in the data I collected for this study. There are 393 players who played in 2010 but who did not play in any of the next three seasons, 2011 through 2013. Of those 393 players, six returned to play in 2014, or about 1.5 percent.

The background variables I took from NFL team rosters (NFL, Team Rosters 2010-14) include date of birth, height, weight, and player position. I computed age based on date of birth and the start date of each respective NFL regular season. I reclassified about twenty player positions into the six-group position variable described in earlier chapters.

STATISTICAL ANALYSIS

For the five-year study period, I calculated descriptive statistics for age, height, and weight. I also provided a frequency distribution for player position based on the six-group classification.

The statistical analysis focuses on the two cohorts of players who played during the 2010 and 2011 regular seasons. I compared career ending among the three groups of players: (1) those on the IRL, (2) those not on the IRL but who missed three or more games following an injury, and (3) all other players. The statistical analysis includes the calculation of odds ratios (ORs) with 95 percent confidence intervals (CIs) by cohort and cohorts combined, comparing the percentage of players in these three groups who ended their careers. An OR of 2, for example, would indicate a doubling of the risk (of career-ending) of one group versus another. Again, 95 percent CIs that exclude the number 1 are significant at the 5 percent level.

RESULTS

I have already presented background variables by study year in table 1-1 of chapter 1. The mean age of players is about twenty-six years. The mean height is very consistent during the study period, averaging about seventy-four inches. The mean weight is about 246 pounds. The most common position type is defensive backs, comprising 33 to 34 percent of all player position types. Offensive backs represent about 13 percent of all position types during the study period, and about 4 percent are kickers.

About 9 to 12 percent of players during each regular season are placed on the IRL. For the focal study years, 2010 and 2011, 226 players (11.7 percent) were placed on the IRL in 2010, and 236 players (12.4 percent) were placed on the IRL in 2011.

Table 8-1 compares the percentage of career ending by cohort and cohorts combined among IRL players (*n* = 226) versus that of injured players not placed on the IRL (*n* = 180). I refer to these groups as "non-IRL injured players" and "all other players" (*n* = 1,520). In 2010, a total of 34.5

percent of IRL players never returned to play in the NFL during any of the next four seasons, and they are considered career-ended. In comparison, 16.1 percent of non-IRL injured players and 18.4 percent of all other players are career-ended. The odds ratios for the IRL versus the non-IRL injured players and the IRL versus all other players are 2.7 and 2.3, respectively. It can be derived that there is about a 2.5-fold significant increase in the risk of career ending in players who are placed on the IRL. The odds ratio for career ending between the two comparison groups was not significant.

As shown in the bottom part of table 8-1, I found similar results in the 2011 cohort. A total of 33.1 percent of 2011 IRL players never returned to play in the NFL during any of the next three seasons (i.e., they ended their careers). This compares to 20.8 percent of non-IRL injured players and 18.1 percent of all other players. The odds ratio is 1.9 for the IRL versus the non-IRL injured players. The odds ratio is 2.2 for the comparison of IRL players to the all other player group. Both of these odds ratios are significant. In other words, there is about a twofold increase in the risk of career ending in players who are placed on the IRL. The odds ratio for the same comparison between non-IRL injured players and all other players is 1.19, which is not significant.

Table 8-2 presents the 2010 and 2011 IRL injury types. Table 8-2 shows a separate frequency distribution for the types of IRL injuries that were linked with players' career ending. I placed injury type with frequencies of less than four into an "other" injury type group. In the distribution for the two cohorts combined, knee injuries are the most common IRL injury type ($n = 128$), composing more than 30 percent of all IRL placements. Besides the "other" group of IRL injuries ($n = 90$), the next-highest injury types are shoulder ($n = 40$), ankle ($n = 36$), hamstring ($n = 32$), and concussion ($n = 26$). In the combined cohorts, nearly three-fourths of the nineteen players with IRL neck injuries ended their careers. Nine of the fifteen players (60 percent) with IRL back/spine injuries and half of the twenty-six players with IRL concussions never returned to play in the NFL.

DISCUSSION

Players placed on the NFL's IRL during two separate seasons (2010 and 2011) have more than double the risk of ending their careers compared to two independent control groups. The two odds ratios for the 2010 IRL players indicate a 2.5-fold increase in the risk of IRL players ending their careers compared to controls. The fact that IRL players may end their careers after experiencing these serious IRL injuries should come as no surprise to most observers. However, the magnitude of this effect had never been studied, and these results add to the existing knowledge on this important subject.

In two separate NFL seasons, about one-third of all IRL players ended their careers following their injuries. In contrast, the percentage of 2010 and 2011 control players who never returned to NFL play ranges from about 16 percent to 21 percent, consistent with reports indicating that players' career length in the NFL is quite short, averaging about 3.3 years (Holstein et al. 2015). The design of this study makes it impossible to conclude that these injuries actually *caused* the excess in career ending among IRL and control players. Additional research is required to examine this possibility in a systematic manner. Beyond the obvious loss of players' careers, IRL injuries may be linked to longer-term pain, disability, and chronic conditions and diseases. There are also obvious financial losses that are associated with career ending.

The results of this study have a great deal of face validity. This includes the significant differences between IRL cases and controls in the percentage of career-ending injuries. While the numbers are small, the results of the types of injuries that are linked to players ending their careers also have face validity. As would be expected, neck injuries, back/spine injuries, and concussions are the IRL injury types that are most likely linked to career ending.

The significant results uncovered in this study seem robust in terms of magnitude and consistency. Additional research is required that more rigorously tests the significant associations uncovered here using a wider range of study variables, as well as improved study design. It is possible that unmeasured variables could be confounding the relationship between IRL placement and career ending.

Concluding Remarks

I expect that a very small percentage of players in this study who were presumed to have ended their careers actually returned or will return to play after missing three to four subsequent seasons. Data presented earlier indicate that about 1.5 percent of eligible players included in this study returned to play after not playing for the previous three years. This percentage would most likely be smaller if four years of data on missed seasons were available. While this extremely small error could fractionally inflate the career-ending percentages presented in this book, I would not have expected it to result in changes to these percentages that would disproportionately affect the three groups I studied.

I noted earlier that changes were made to the IRL rules beginning in 2012. Since then, each team has had the option of designating one player per season as eligible for return that season. This study focuses on the two cohorts of players who played in the 2010 and 2011 regular seasons.

About 89 percent of all NFL games are covered in the weekly injury reports. The missing 11 percent would deflate the number of non-IRL injuries uncovered in this study. However, this systematic bias would not be expected to disproportionately impact the three groups studied here with respect to career ending.

Few would dispute the fact that IRL injuries are very serious for affected NFL players and their families, teams, owners, and fans. In addition to potential short-term pain and disability, players may have to end playing football for at least the rest of the season. According to this study, more than one-third of IRL players will never return to playing football in the NFL again. While not examined in this paper, it seems likely that some of these injuries will result in long-term chronic conditions that impact quality of life and functioning. Prevention of these serious injuries requires attention and prioritization at the highest levels of the league.

REFERENCES

Boublik, M., T. F. Schlegel, R. C. Koonce, J. W. Genuario, and J. D. Kinkartz. 2013. "Quadriceps Tendon Injuries in National Football League Players." *American Journal of Sports Medicine* 41 (8): 1841–6.

Boublik, M., T. Schlegel, R. Koonce, J. Genuario, C. Lind, and D. Hamming. 2011. "Patellar Tendon Ruptures in National Football League Players." *American Journal of Sports Medicin* 39 (11): 2436–40.

Erickson, B. J., J. D. Harris, J. R. Heninger, R. Frank, C. A. Bush-Joseph, N. N. Verma, B. J. Cole, and B. R. Bach. 2014. "Performance and Return to Sport after ACL Reconstruction in NFL Quarterbacks." *Orthopedics* 37 (8): 728–34.

ESPN. 2010–2014. "NFL Transactions." http://espn.go.com/nfl/transactions.

Holstein, J. A., R. S. Jones, and G. E. Koonce Jr. 2015. "Is There Life after Football? Surviving the NFL." New York: New York University Press.

Hsu, W. K. I, K. J. McCarthy, J. W. Savage, D. W. Roberts, G. C. Roc, A. J. Micev, M. A. Terry, S. M. Gryzlo, and M. F. Schafer. 2011. "The Professional Athlete Spine Initiative: Outcomes after Lumbar Disc Herniation in 342 Elite Professional Athletes." *Spine Journal.* 11 (3):180–6.

Lynch, T. S., M. D. Saltzman, J. H. Ghodasra, K. Y. Bilimoria, M. K. Bowen, and G. W. Nuber. 2013. "Acromioclavicular Joint Injuries in the National Football League: Epidemiology and Management." *American Journal of Sports Medicine* 41 (12): 2904–8.

Mansour, A. A. III, J. W. Genuario, J. P. Young, T. P. Murphy, M. Boublik, and T. F. Schlegel. 2013. "National Football League Athletes' Return to Play after Surgical Reattachment of Complete Proximal Hamstring Ruptures." *American Journal of Orthopedics* 42 (6).

Maske, M. "Players' Union Approves Changes to NFL's Injured Reserve Rule, Trade Deadline." 2012. Washington Post, Insider, August 20. http://www.washingtonpost.com/blogs/football-insider/wp/2012/08/30/players-union-approves-changes to nfls-injured-reserve-rule-trade-deadline/.

Miller, J. "Stone Johnson Died 50 Years Ago from Injury in NFL Game." 2013. *USA Today* online, August 31. http://www.usatoday.com/story/sports/nfl/2013/08/29/nfl-player-death-anniversary-stone-johnson-len-dawson-chiefs/2735393/.

Mueller, F. O., and R. C. Cantu. 2011. "Football Fatalities and Catastrophic Injuries, 1931–2008." Durham, NC: Carolina Academic Press.

NFL. 2010–2014a. "Game Logs." http://www.nfl.com/player/ gamelogs.

———. 2010–2014b. "Injury Reports" http://www.nfl.com/injuries.

———. 2010–2014c. "Team Rosters." http://www.nfl.com/players/search?category=name.

———. 2010–2014d. "Transactions" http://www.nfl.com/transactions.

Table 8-1. Career Ending among 2010 and 2011 IRL Players versus Two Comparison Groups

			Career Ended (did not play 2011-14)			
	2010 Players		Yes		No	
Three-Group Classification	N	%	N	%	N	%
1. IRL	226	11.7%	78	34.5%	148	63.5%
2. Missed 3+ Games Following a Non-IRL Injury	180	9.4%	29	16.1%	151	83.9%
3. All Remaining Other	1,520	78.9%	280	18.4%	1,240	81.6%

Statistical Results (2010)		
Pairwise Comparisons (between Groups 1,2 and 3 above)	Odd Ratio (95% CI)	p-value
Group 1 versus Group 2	2.7 (1.7, 4.4)	< 0.0001
Group 1 versus Group 3	2.3 (1.7, 3.2)	<0.0001
Group 2 versus Group 3	0.9 (0.6, 1.3)	0.4477

			Career Ended (did not play 2012-14)			
	2011 Players		Yes		No	
Three-Group Classification	N	%	N	%	N	%
1. IRL	236	12.4%	78	33.1%	158	67.0%
2. Missed 3+ Games Following a Non-IRL Injury	216	11.3%	45	20.8%	171	79.2%
3. All Remaining Other	1,458	76.3%	264	18.1%	1,194	81.9%

Statistical Results (2011)		
Pairwise Comparisons (between Groups 1,2 and 3 above)	Odd Ratio (95% CI)	p-value
Group 1 versus Group 2	1.9 (1.2, 2.9)	0.0038
Group 1 versus Group 3	2.2 (1.6, 3.0)	<0.0001
Group 2 versus Group 3	1.2 (0.8, 1.7)	0.3356

	Table 8-2. IRL Injury Types and Career Ending among NFL Players							
	2010				2011			
	All IRL Injuries		IRL Injury Coincided with Career Ending		All IRL Injuries		IRL Injury Coincided with Career Ending	
IRL Type Injury	N	%	N	%	N	%	N	%
Achilles	5	2.2%	1	1.3%	8	3.4%	1	1.3%
Ankle	17	7.5%	3	3.9%	19	8.1%	5	6.4%
Back/spine	5	2.2%	3	3.9%	10	4.2%	6	7.7%
Concussion	10	4.4%	4	5.1%	16	6.8%	9	11.4%
Foot	8	3.5%	3	3.9%	15	6.4%	3	3.9%
Groin	7	3.1%	2	2.6%	2	0.9%	1	1.3%
Hamstring	17	7.5%	8	10.3%	15	6.4%	4	5.1%
Hip	6	2.7%	1	1.3%	4	1.7%	1	1.3%
Knee	70	31.0%	24	30.8%	58	24.6%	18	23.1%
Leg	5	2.2%	1	1.3%	7	3.0%	1	1.3%
Neck	11	4.9%	8	10.3%	8	3.4%	6	7.7%
Shoulder	25	11.1%	11	14.1%	15	6.4%	6	7.7%
Toe	5	2.2%	0	0.0%	4	1.7%	1	1.3%
Other	35	15.5%	9	11.4%	55	23.3%	16	20.5%
Total	226	100.0%	78	100.0%	236	100.0%	78	100.0%

CHAPTER 9

Five-Year Outcomes of Players
Selected in the 2010 NFL Draft

• • •

THIS BOOK HAS EXAMINED A range of outcomes among NFL players, usually for a five-year study period, 2010 through 2014. The players selected in the 2010 NFL Draft have a number of things in common:

1. None of them had ever played before in the NFL.
2. In 2015, when this book was written, five years had passed since all of these players had been drafted.
3. The large majority of these draftees are about the same age.

Collectively, these factors make these players an ideal group to follow to determine aspects of their careers, issues they have on and off the playing field, and injury-related outcomes during the five-year period since being drafted.

Previous chapters have examined a range of outcomes separately. For example, there are specific chapters on arrests, physical fines, suspensions, and the career consequences of being placed on the IRL. None of the previous chapters, however, have examined a *range* of outcomes on a particular player sample.

It is certainly possible that players drafted in 2010 suffered serious injuries or were involved in problems with the law during their lives and careers preceding their careers in the NFL. All drafted players, however, begin their NFL careers with a "clean slate" within the league. This chapter describes a five-year natural history of the 2010 draftees as they proceeded through their careers and lives on and off the playing field. I assessed a total of eight outcomes in three categories over a five-year study period for all 2010 draftees. In this chapter, I also examine the relationship between players' placement in the draft and the eight outcome variables.

METHODS

All 255 players selected in the 2010 NFL Draft are eligible for this study. There are, however, nineteen players who were drafted in 2010 but never played a regular-season game in the NFL. In effect, then, the study sample includes the 236 players selected in the 2010 NFL Draft who played in the league during one to five regular seasons. Twenty-nine players selected in the 2010 NFL Draft did not play in the 2010 regular season but did play in at least one of the four study seasons after that. These players are included in the analyses for this chapter.

The background variables are age, draft-pick number and round, and position. I provide mean age and draft-pick numbers of the 2010 draftees and give frequency distributions for draft round and the three- and six-group-position variables used previously in this book. I display the number of draftees who played in the NFL regular seasons for each of the five study years and for the seasons combined. I also show a frequency distribution of total number of years played.

I studied a total of eight outcomes encompassing three categories: career, trouble, and injuries. Career outcomes include (1) playing a limited number of regular seasons in the NFL, (2) career interruption, and (3) career ending. I counted draftees who played in only one or two regular seasons (out of a maximum of five) as having a limited number of seasons played. I counted a career as being interrupted if a player missed one or more regular seasons during the five-year study period and then returned to the league for one or more additional seasons. I considered a career ended if a player failed to appear in any regular-season games during the last two, three, or four study years (2013–14, 2012–14, or 2011–14). I did not count players as ending their careers if they miss the 2014 season only because a significant minority of players return to play in the league after missing a single season. The same is not generally the case for players who miss two or more years in the league. I also did not count players who ended their careers as having interrupted careers.

A second category is made up of arrests, physical fines, and suspensions, which I refer to as "trouble" outcomes. These refer to trouble with the law or the league, usually off the playing field (i.e., arrests and/or suspensions) and/or trouble with the league on the field in the form of physical fines. I use the same methods as were described in chapters 2–5, 6, and 7 to measure arrests, suspensions, and physical fines, respectively.

Concussions and IRL placement (for any injury type) make up the third category of outcomes: injuries. I obtained concussion data from both the NFL Injury Report (NFL, Injury Reports 2010–14) and the NFL Injured Reserve List (IRL) (NFL, Transactions 2010–14) for the regular seasons of interest. I obtained IRL data using the methods described in chapter 8.

I provide the number and percentage of 2010 draftees who experienced each of the three outcomes for the combined five-year study period. I also give the number and percentage of draftees who are arrested, fined for physical violations, or suspended for each of the five years and all years combined. I have done the same for the two injury-related outcomes: concussions and IRL placement. I computed the number and percentage of unique draftees experiencing any of the three career outcomes. Similarly, I calculated the number and percentage of unique drafted players who had any of the three "trouble" outcomes and did the same for the two injury variables. Finally, I provided the number and percentage of unique players with any of the eight outcomes.

RESULTS

In the 2010 Draft, 255 players were selected. Because nineteen of them never played in a regular-season NFL game, I dropped them from the analysis. Many of these individuals played in the NFL during the 2010 preseason but failed to ever make a regular-season roster. This leaves 236 players to serve as the basis of the analysis. See table 9-1. With respect to background variables, these remaining 236 players have a mean age of 22.5 years. Most of the players (n = 192; 81.4 percent) were either twenty-two or twenty-three years old in 2010. Slightly more defensive players (n = 129; 54.7 percent) are among the 236 draftees compared to 105 (44.5 percent) offensive players. There are two kickers among the 2010 draftees. The mean draft pick number of the 236 players included in this analysis is 121.9.

A total of 207 players got drafted and actually played in the NFL in 2010. Between 2011 and 2014, a total of 194, 186, 160, and 143 of these individuals played in the respective regular seasons. Of the 255 players drafted in 2010, a total of 143 (56.1 percent) played in 2014. This does not, however, mean that these 143 individuals played during all five study years. Nearly half of the 236 draftees included in the analysis (n = 115; 48.7 percent) did play in all five regular seasons. Smaller but consistent numbers and percentages of 2010 draftees played in one, two, three, or four regular seasons (n = 27, 11.4 percent; n = 30, 12.7 percent; n = 28, 11.9 percent; n = 36, 15.3 percent), respectively.

Table 9-2 shows the results as detailed outcomes. With respect to career outcomes, five-year combined results are given. A total of fifty-seven of the 2010 draftees (24.2 percent) played in one or two of the five regular seasons studied, twenty-six players (11.0 percent) had interrupted careers, and sixty-five (27.5 percent) ended their careers. A total of ninety-three (39.4 percent) of the 236 draftees (39.4 percent) had at least one of the three career outcomes.

The results for the trouble outcomes are shown in the middle of table 9-2 for each of the five years and for all years combined. About one of every eleven of the 2010 draftees (8.9 percent) were arrested at least once during the five study years combined. Nearly one of every five of the draftees (18.9 percent) received at least one fine for a physical offense, and fourteen (5.9 percent) were suspended by the league at least once. More than one of every four draftees (26.7 percent) had at least one of the three trouble outcomes during the five-year study period.

The results for the injury outcomes are shown toward the bottom of table 9-2 for each study year and for all the years combined. IRL placements were highest in 2011 (15.5 percent), and concussions peaked in 2013 (8.8 percent). More than half of all 2010 draftees (52.1 percent) were placed on the IRL and/or suffered at least one concussion during the five-year study period.

Nearly 84 percent of the 2010 draftees experienced at least one of the eight outcome variables included in this chapter for the five-year study period combined.

Table 9-3 shows that there are significant relationships among six of the study outcomes and the draft-pick number. However, the directionality of these relationships varies with the type of outcome. Players with any of the three career outcomes have a mean in the 147–154 range as far as draft-pick numbers, compared to average numbers in the 112–118 range among players who did not experience these career outcomes. On the other hand, the mean draft-pick number is significantly lower (i.e., earlier round picks) for draftees who were arrested or received a fine for a physical violation. The third trouble outcome, suspension, has similar results to the two other variables but fails to reach significance. Players who experienced concussions have a mean draft-pick number of 97.6, which is significantly lower than draftees who did not have concussions.

Discussion

This chapter follows 2010 draftees on a range of on- and off-field outcomes for a five-year period of time. This is a long time in the NFL, in which entire careers are believed to average just 3.3 years (Holstein et al. 2015). In brief, the results documented in this chapter indicate that during the five-year study period, about 39 percent of draftees had at least one of the career outcomes, 26.7 percent had one or more trouble outcomes, and 52.1 percent had at least one of the injury outcomes. In all, nearly 84 percent of the draftees experienced at least one of the eight outcomes during the five-year study period. Draft-pick number and six of the eight outcome variables are statistically related. However, sometimes draft-pick number is consistently lower for some outcomes and consistently higher for others. The careers of NFL players can be impacted by injuries, intense competition, and a host of other factors. As one veteran NFL player notes, "There will always be replacements on the horizon. There is no team where that isn't the case. You have to fight for your job throughout your career" (NESN 2015). While NFL veterans may feel career uncertainty about their futures, players in the league for just a few years also face unknown, and sometimes volatile, futures in the league. This may be especially true for marginal players who get selected in the later rounds of the draft, as well as those who sign as free agents. Career havoc and uncertainty are reflected in the career-outcome findings documented in this chapter. Significant minorities of 2010 draftees played only one or two of the five regular seasons, had interrupted careers, or have already ended their NFL careers. In all, nearly four of ten of the 2010 draftees suffered at least one of these three career outcomes during the relatively brief five-year study period.

On a positive note, nearly half of all 2010 draftees played all five regular seasons studied. In post hoc analysis, draftees who played in all five regular seasons are compared to the combined group of individuals who played in one to four seasons. The draftees with five years of playing experience have a mean draft-pick number of 99.1, compared to 143.7 for the draftees who played one to four seasons. This difference is statistically significant. As expected, the more highly regarded draftees play more NFL seasons. (Table display is not shown for data in this paragraph.)

In fact, there is considerable variability in the nature of the draftees' careers. Table 9-4 illustrates the "patterns" of regular seasons played by the 2010 draftees between 2010 and 2014. The pattern column contains either a zero (did not play) or one (played) for each of the five seasons respectively. For example, a player with a "11110" pattern played all regular seasons between 2010 and 2013 but did not play in 2014. A player with a pattern of "10100" played in 2010 and 2012 but did not play in 2011, 2013, or 2014.

The 236 players drafted in 2010 have twenty-four different career patterns between 2010 and 2014. This means that on average, for every ten players drafted in 2010, there is one different career pattern for individuals in the league during a five-year period. As this follow-up period lengthens, there will certainly be new career patterns emerging, and a larger proportion of players will be affected by the career outcomes examined in this chapter. The fact that just under 40 percent of all draftees have experienced one or more of the specific career outcomes seems high, although no comparison group is used in this chapter. Future studies can examine the rates of these career outcomes for other draft classes.

All career outcomes are associated with draft-pick number in a consistent manner. Players selected in the later rounds of the draft are significantly more likely to experience shorter and interrupted careers and are also more likely to have already ended their careers. In general, there is a difference of about thirty to forty draft-pick numbers between those who do and do not experience each of the three career outcomes, and this seems logical. Players selected in the later rounds of the draft may not be as high-quality football players as individuals drafted in the earlier rounds. Logically, the intense competition embodied in the NFL would have more impact on the careers of marginal players.

Any player who makes an NFL team, or is even considered for one, has to be very talented. Nevertheless, there are many levels of talent, and early-round draft picks are likely to be at the highest end of the talent spectrum. It should come as no surprise that the nineteen players drafted in 2010 who never made a regular roster in the NFL had a mean draft-pick number higher than two hundred. With the exception of one player drafted as number seventy-six, the other eighteen players who never made the regular roster were picked at number 152 and above. The player drafted as number seventy-six was involved in a car accident in 2010 that resulted in a dozen surgeries and the end of his NFL career (Wesseling 2013).

More than one-fourth (26.7 percent) of the players drafted in 2010 were involved in at least one of the trouble outcomes, which include arrests, suspensions, and physical fines. In post hoc analyses, I compared the incidence rates of each of the three trouble outcomes during the five-year study period for the 2010 draftees to the overall 2010–14 regular-season populations analyzed in the previous chapters. These incidence rates are virtually identical. These computations are not stratified by age, however, and virtually all of the 2010 draftees would be in the youngest age group (twenty-four years and younger) or the next youngest group (twenty-five to twenty-seven years) during the latter years of this study. Without additional analyses, no real conclusions can be reached with confidence regarding the incidence rates of the trouble outcomes in this chapter. On a very cursory basis, however, the trouble-incidence rates of 2010 draftees seem consistent with the overall population of NFL players during the five-year study period.

The relationships between the trouble outcomes presented in this chapter and draft-pick number are significant for arrests and physical fines. The suspension results are very similar to the other two trouble outcomes but fail to be significant, probably due to the relatively small number of suspensions observed in this sample. The results for all three trouble outcomes are very consistent with respect to the mean draft-pick numbers, which average about 87 for players who experience any of the trouble items, and between 125 and 130 for those who do not. In other words, the players with arrests, suspensions, and physical fines are generally the better football players selected earlier in the 2010 NFL Draft. Holstein and colleagues (2015) talk about the "dark side" of being considered a special athlete in regard to elite college football players. Expectations tend to run high for these athletes: "The darker side of such expectations, however, is that elite athletes sometimes lose sight of conventions, rules, and regulations by which most everyone else abides… Sometimes flaunting the rules leads elite athletes to run amok legally" (Holstein et al. 2015, 36).

Additional research is required to better understand why the most highly regarded elite NFL players are more likely to get into trouble both on and off the playing field.

Is it possible that the players drafted the earliest are also the ones with troubled histories before beginning their NFL careers? In the months, weeks, and even days leading up to the 2015 NFL Draft, at least three of the projected first- and second-round draft picks were arrested (Herndon 2015; Goodbread 2015; Yuscavage 2015). Charges against these players include marijuana possession (Herndon 2015), driving under the influence (Goodbread 2015), and domestic violence (Yuscavage 2015). These three players may have dropped lower in the draft because of these issues, but were all selected no worse than seventy-eight. Also, the top overall pick in the 2015 NFL Draft faced sexual-assault charges from an incident that allegedly occurred in 2012 (AP 2015). Finally, a top-five projected selection in the 2016 draft was recently arrested for domestic violence (Cooper 2015). These data provide anecdotal evidence that some of the most recent highly regarded draftees have arrest histories that precede the start of their NFL careers. The league must monitor these players and their teams carefully to prevent recidivist behavior during their professional careers.

The two injury outcomes, IRL placement and concussions, are unrelated to each other. Although twenty-three players had at least one IRL placement plus at least one concussion, only four of these IRL injury types were concussions. I expected this number to be small because very few concussions actually result in IRL placement. There are more IRL placements ($n = 91$) among 2010 draftees during the five-year study period than any of the other seven outcomes. The next-highest incidence outcome is career ending, with sixty-five players. In fact, twenty-one of the ninety-one draftees (23.1 percent) with IRL placements also ended their careers (data not shown).

In this study, nearly one of every four of the 2010 draftees had at least one concussion. Draftees who experienced concussions had a mean draft-pick number of 97.6, versus 129.3 for players without a concussion, which is a statistically significant difference (see table 9-5). My previous book, *Pigskin Crossroads: The Epidemiology of Concussions in the National Football League, 2010–12*, shows a significant exposure response relationship. In other words, the more games played, the greater the risk of concussion. In post hoc analysis, I compared the mean number of player games during the five-year study period for 2010 draftees with and without concussions. Each time a player participated in a regular-season game, I added one player game. So a player who played ten games in 2010 and fourteen during 2011 had twenty-four player games for these two seasons combined. Players drafted in 2010 who had at least one concussion during the five-year study period played an average of 53.8 player games in total, compared to 42.3 games for players without concussions. These results indicate that playing more games is likely to increase the risk of concussions. This result is consistent with exposure-response results for concussions presented in my previous book (Markowitz and Markowitz 2013).

Returning for a moment to one of the trouble results, the draft-pick number for players with physical fines is more than forty numbers lower than those without physical fines (see table 9-3). Getting physical fines may also be related to exposure response because these are actions that usually occur on the playing field. (Most suspensions are due to off-field violations like PEDs and substance abuse.) Hence, more time spent on the playing field is likely to be associated with more physical fines. This turns out to be the case in another post hoc analysis. Players with at least one physical fine for the five study years have a mean of 63.6 player games, versus 40.6 for draftees without any physical fines.

Concluding Remarks

The natural history and outcomes of NFL draftees' careers and lives have never been studied before. The material presented in this chapter can lay the groundwork for future studies in this area. Clearly, NFL players' careers and lives can be uncertain. The intense competition for jobs and player injuries definitely play a role in this. Yet a substantial number of 2010 draftees, nearly half, have managed to play in all five regular seasons. This is, however, more likely to be the case in players drafted early. On the other hand, adverse career outcomes are more likely to occur in more marginal players selected in the later rounds of the draft. Interestingly, players selected early in the draft are more likely to experience trouble outcomes.

REFERENCES

Associated Press. 2015. "NFL's Top Draft Pick Denies Rape Allegations." May 9. http://nypost.com/2015/05/09/jameis-winston-denies-rape-allegations-in-counter-suit-against-accuser/.

Cooper, J. 2015. "Ole Miss OT Laremy Tunsil Arrested for Hitting Stepfather, Defending Mother" June 27. http://www.saturdaydownsouth.com/ole-miss-football/laremy-tunsil-arrested-2015/.

Goodbread, C. 2015. "Florida State Prospect P. J. Williams Arrested on DUI Charge" NFL: Path to the Draft. http://www.nfl.com/news/story/0ap3000000483385/article/florida-state-prospect-pj-williams-arrested-on-dui-charge.

Herndon, M. 2015. "Projected 1st-round NFL draft pick Shane Ray arrested for marijuana possession" AL.com, April 27. http://www.al.com/sports/index.ssf/2015/04/projected_1st-round_nfl_draft.html.

Holstein, J. A., R. S. Jones, and G. E. Koonce Jr. 2015. "Is There Life after Football? Surviving the NFL." New York: New York University Press.

Markowitz, J. S. and A. Markowitz. 2013. *Pigskin Crossroads: The Epidemiology of Concussions in the National Football League, 2010–12.* CreateSpace.

NESN. "Brady Poppinga: Draft creates uncertainty for veteran NFL players." May 4, 2015, http://nesn.com/2015/05/brady-poppinga-draft-creates-uncertainty-for-veteran-nfl-players/.

NFL. "Injury Reports [for Week 17, 2014]." http://www.nfl.com/injuries?week=17.

NFL. "Transactions." http://www.nfl.com/transactions

Wesseling, A. 2013. "Chad Jones will try baseball after failed NFL comeback" NFL, May 9. http://www.nfl.com/news/story/0ap1000000168337/article/chad-jones-will-try-baseball-after-failed-nfl-comeback.

Yuscavage, C. 2015. "Seahawks Criticized for Selecting Former Michigan Player Frank Clark in NFL Draft Despite Domestic Violence-Related Arrest" Complex Sports, May 5. http://www.complex.com/sports/2015/05/seahawks-criticized-selecting-frank-clark-nfl-draft-domestic-violence-arrest.

Table 9-1. Background Variables for 236 Players Selected in 2010 NFL Draft Who Played One+ Regular Seasons between 2010 and 2014

Variables		
Mean Age (years)	22.5	
Draft Round Selected	N	%
1	32	13.6
2	32	13.6
3	33	14.0
4	33	14.0
5	36	15.3
6	31	13.1
7	39	16.5
Mean Draft Pick*	121.9	
Position	N	%
Three-Group		
Offense	105	44.5
Defense	129	54.7
Kicking	2	0.9
Six-Group		
Offensive back	24	10.2
Offensive line	35	14.8
Receiver	46	19.5
Defensive back	76	32.2
Defensive line	53	22.5
Kicking	2	0.9

Table 9-2. Number and Percentage of 2010 NFL Draftees Who Experienced Career, "Trouble," and Injury Outcomes, 2010–14

	2010		2011		2012		2013		2014		2010–14 Combined	
	n=207		n=194		n=186		n=160		n=143		n=236	
Outcome Variables	N	%	N	%	N	%	N	%	N	%	N	%
A. Career Outcomes												
Played Two Regular Seasons or Less				Not applicable							57	24.2
Career Ended											65	27.5
Interrupted Career											26	11.0
1+ of the Career Outcomes Above											93	39.4
B. "Trouble" Outcomes												
Arrest	5	2.4	4	2.1	2	2.2	8	5.0	4	2.8	21	8.9
Physical Fine	7	3.4	11	5.7	15	8.1	23	14.4	12	8.4	44	18.6
Suspension	2	0.97	4	2.1	5	2.7	2	1.3	2	1.4	14	5.9
1+ of the "Trouble" Outcomes Above				Not calculated							63	26.7
C. Injury Outcomes												
IRL	19	9.2	30	15.5	24	12.9	20	12.5	14	9.8	91	38.6
Concussion	15	7.3	16	8.4	15	8.1	14	8.8	8	5.6	55	23.3
1+ of the Injury Outcomes Above				Not calculated							123	52.1
1+ of Any Outcome Above				Not calculated							198	83.9

Table 9-3. Statistical Comparison of Mean Draft-Pick Numbers of 2010 NFL Draftees by Eight Outcome Variables

Outcome Variables				
A. Career Outcomes				
1. Played One or Two Seasons (Only)	N	Mean Draft-Pick Number	t-statistic	p-value
Yes	57	154.2	4.0	< 0.0001
No	179	111.7		
2. Career Interrupted				
Yes	26	146.7	2.1	0.0407
No	205	118.2		
3. Career Ended				
Yes	65	149.2	3.7	0.0003
No	171	111.6		
B. "Trouble" Outcomes				
1. Arrested				
Yes	21	86.6	2.4	0.0188
No	215	125.4		
2. Physical Fine				
Yes	44	87.7	3.6	0.0004
No	192	129.8		
3. Suspension				
Yes	14	87.2	1.9	0.064
No	222	124.1		
C. Injury Outcomes				
1. IRL Placement				
Yes	91	115.2	1.1	0.2551
No	145	126.2		
2. Concussion				
Yes	55	97.6	2.9	0.0042
No	181	129.3		

Table 9-4. Number of 2010 Draftees with Various Career Patterns of Play in 2010–14 NFL Regular Seasons					
	Regular-Season				
Pattern*	2010	2011	2012	2013	2014
01001	0	1	0	0	1
01011	0	1	0	1	1
10001	2	0	0	0	2
10011	1	0	0	1	1
10101	2	0	2	0	2
10110	3	0	3	3	0
10111	4	0	4	4	4
11001	1	1	0	0	1
11010	3	3	0	3	0
11011	3	3	0	3	3
11101	5	5	5	0	5
10100	5	0	5	0	0
00100	0	0	3	0	0
00110	0	0	2	2	0
00111	0	0	3	3	3
01000	0	7	0	0	0
01100	0	6	6	0	0
01110	0	1	1	1	0
01111	0	5	5	5	5
10000	17	0	0	0	0
11000	14	14	0	0	0
11100	13	13	13	0	0
11110	19	19	19	19	0
11111	115	115	115	115	115
* 0 = did not play, 1 = did play in 2010–14 regular seasons respectively					

Part Four
Mortality

• • •

CHAPTER 10

Risk Factors of Mortality in a Twenty-Seven-Year NFL Cohort (1960–86)

● ● ●

ON AVERAGE, PROFESSIONAL FOOTBALL PLAYERS are large in physical size. They participate in a violent game that could impact their well-being, both on and off of the playing field. In recent times, more than two-thirds of NFL players have been African American (*USA Today* Sports 2014), and nearly half of all current players in the league were born in the Southern part of the United States (Kacsmar 2013). These factors, alone or in combination, may impact players' well-being, and even their mortality, years after their football careers are over. The study of mortality in special populations, like retired professional football players, can add to the existing knowledge on risk and protective factors and can lead to prevention efforts aimed at extending life and improving its quality. Such knowledge could benefit those participating in football and may also have implications for the general population.

This chapter examines several potential risk factors for mortality in a large cohort of NFL players who played in the league between 1960 and 1986. The literature review for this chapter begins with a brief description of selected risk factors for mortality in the general population, including variables like age, race, body mass index, and birthplace. Following that, the literature review focuses on studies of mortality of NFL players.

GENERAL-POPULATION LITERATURE REVIEW: SELECT RISK FACTORS FOR MORTALITY

There is extensive literature that identifies demographic and other risk and protective factors for mortality in the US general population. The following sections briefly describe this literature as it relates to several of the variables studied in this chapter.

AGE AND MORTALITY

The factor that best predicts mortality, in any general population, is age. With just a few important exceptions, a person's chances of dying increases as he or she gets older. Infant mortality (i.e., deaths) that occur during the first year of life is one of these exceptions. This first year of life poses a number of special risks like birth defects, preterm birth, and maternal complications during pregnancy, that result in higher death rates compared to later years. In the United States, once a child survives the first year of life, the risk of dying drops precipitously during years one through fourteen. Death rates then begin to rise at fifteen to thirty-four years and generally continue to ascend in successive years (CDC 2014).

Mortality rates and life expectancy can vary dramatically based on a wide range of factors. In some African countries, for example, life expectancy at birth can be less than fifty years of age. In other countries, like Japan, Canada, Australia, and several Western European countries, the average life expectancy exceeds eighty years (World Health Organization 2015). Public health measures, diet, education, tobacco and alcohol use, occupational and environmental exposures, physical activity/inactivity, gender, race, economic circumstances, and many other factors can help account for these differences (Fletcher et al. 2013).

RACE AND MORTALITY

In general, death rates in the United States have fallen in recent years. Nevertheless, disparities in mortality between African American and white adults in the general population continue to be documented in the scientific literature (Woolf et al. 2004). Between 1960 and 2000, death rates were, on average, 40 to 50 percent higher in African Americans than whites (Satcher et al. 2005). This disparity in death rates has worsened for African American men during this forty-year period. Standardized mortality ratios (SMRs) for African American versus white men rose from 1.38 in 1960 to 1.49 in the year 2000. In other words, the risk of dying for African Americans was 38 percent and 49 percent higher than it was for whites during these years. In 1990, there was a 59 percent increased risk of dying among African American versus white men (Satcher et al. 2005). Wong and colleagues (2002) found that the diseases/conditions that are responsible for the largest disparities between African Americans and whites in potential life years lost are cardiovascular disease (33 percent), HIV/AIDS (11.2 percent), trauma (10.7 percent), and diabetes mellitus (8.5 percent) (Wong et al. 2002). The 2010 Healthy People Initiative set as its primary goal the elimination of these and other health disparities (Department of Health and Human Services 2000).

Body Mass Index and Mortality

Several studies indicate that more than two-thirds of all American men aged twenty years and older are overweight or obese (Flegal et al. 2010; Ogden et al. 2006). Based on data collected between 1999 and 2008, the percentage of overweight and obese people in the United States increases with age, averaging 63.5 percent in males between twenty and thirty-nine years of age, 77.8 percent in men aged forty to fifty-nine years, and over 78 percent in men over the age of sixty (Flegal et al. 2010). Obesity, based on a BMI of at least thirty, is prevalent in more than 32 percent of males who are twenty years of age and older and increases with each of the age groups, rising from 27.5 percent in twenty- to thirty-nine-year-olds, to 34.3 percent in the forty- to fifty-nine-year-old group, and 37.1 percent in men age sixty and older (Flegal et al. 2010).

Convincing literature exists on the relationship between BMI and mortality. In general, obese adults have higher death rates than normal-weight adults. In one study, for example, obese adults have death rates that are at least 20 percent higher than normal-weight adults for both all-cause mortality and cardiovascular disease (CVD) (Borrell and Samuel 2014). Deaths due to all-cause mortality is advanced by 3.7 years within groups with the highest levels of obesity (Borrell and Samuel 2014).

Berrington de Gonzalez and colleagues (2010) retrieved pooled BMI/mortality data from nineteen prospective studies. In all, they studied the information on nearly 1.5 million white males and females to determine the relationship between BMI and all-cause mortality. They found that within healthy men who never smoked, hazard ratios for mortality rise significantly in individuals with BMIs over thirty, compared to normal BMIs. Those males with the very highest BMIs, in excess of thirty-five, have about two to three times the risk of dying relative to men with normal BMIs (Berrington de Gonzalez et al. 2010).

Birthplace and Mortality

According to the Robert Wood Johnson Foundation, birthplace is a significant predictor of life expectancy. Data this organization compiled indicate how babies born in different places—even when they are in the same state but different cities just a few miles apart—can have life expectancies that differ by as much as twenty-five years (Robert Wood Johnston Foundation 2013). In fact, many of the states with the highest death rates are located in the southern part of the United States. In 2013, the states with the highest number of deaths per hundred thousand population were Mississippi (960), Alabama (925), West Virginia (924), Oklahoma (911), Kentucky (900), Louisiana (898), Arkansas (894), Tennessee (881), South Carolina (838), and Indiana (832) (Centers for Disease Control 2014). The first nine states listed are located in the southern region of the United States based on published Census divisions (US Census Bureau 2015).

In brief, older age, African American race, obesity, and birth in the southern region of the United States are established risk factors for mortality in the US general population.

LITERATURE REVIEW: NFL MORTALITY STUDIES

Most of what is currently known about mortality among NFL players is derived from three studies conducted by the National Institute of Occupational Safety and Health (NIOSH) researchers. NIOSH is a part of the US Centers for Disease Control and Prevention (CDC) within the US Department of Health and Human Services. Briefly, NIOSH conducts research aimed at minimizing and reducing work-related injury and illness. The three NIOSH mortality studies of retired NFL players are in the forms of (1) a letter to the NFLPA written in 1994 (NIOSH Letter to NFLPA 1994), (2) a journal article in the *American Journal of Cardiology* focusing on mortality and cardiovascular diseases (Baron et al. 2012), and (3) a journal article in *Neurology* focusing on mortality and neurodegenerative causes (Lehman et al. 2012). The players followed in these three studies consist of samples of individuals who played in the NFL between 1959 and 1988.

The statistics used in the three NIOSH mortality studies generally involve two types of analyses: (1) comparisons between NFL players' mortality experience and that of the US general population and (2) internal comparisons of players based on factors like player position and playing-time BMI. The comparisons with the US population are accomplished using the NIOSH life table analysis system (Schubauer-Berigan et al. 2011), which generates standardized mortality ratios (SMRs) of all cause- and disease-specific player mortality versus that of the US general population.

THE 1994 NIOSH LETTER

The key findings of the NIOSH mortality studies reported in 1994 include the following:

1. There was a total of 139 deaths among 6,848 NFL players (about 2 percent) who played in the league between 1959 and 1988. These players were followed through December 31, 1991, to determine whether they were deceased or alive.

2. Overall mortality risk is significantly *decreased* among NFL players compared to the US general population.

3. The risk of death due to violence or accidents is substantially decreased among NFL players versus the general population.

4. There is a nonsignificant increased risk of neurodegenerative deaths among NFL players compared to the general population.

5. There is a near-significant increased risk of deaths from CVD among NFL linemen (versus other position categories).

6. Nonwhite NFL players have a significantly higher risk of all-cause death compared to whites.

7. NFL players with the highest playing-time BMIs have a significantly higher risk of death compared to players with the lowest BMIs.

THE 2012 FOLLOW-UP NIOSH MORTALITY STUDIES

The follow-up mortality studies, published in 2012 by Baron and colleagues (2012) and Lehman et al. (2012), use many of the same methods as the original 1994 NIOSH report. However, they focus more specifically on deaths due to cardiovascular and neurological causes. Moreover, the 2012 studies follow players' vital status sixteen years longer than the 1994 NIOSH report does. Hence, there are more deaths to incorporate into the analyses in the 2012 studies.

The key findings of the Baron et al. study (2012) based on a vital-status end date of December 31, 2007, include the following:

1. There are a total of 334 deaths among 3,429 NFL players (9.7 percent).

2. Overall mortality risk is significantly *decreased* among NFL players compared to the US general population.

3. The risk of death from cancer is significantly decreased among NFL players versus the general population.

4. There is a significant decreased risk of CVD deaths among NFL players compared to the general population.

5. The risk of death from CVD is significantly increased for defensive linemen versus other positions.
6. Nonwhite NFL players have a significantly higher risk of all-cause death than white players.
7. NFL players with the highest playing-time BMIs have a significantly higher risk of death than players with lower BMIs.

Lehman and colleagues (2012) studied the same exact 3,429 players as Baron et al. and also report the same decreased overall mortality risk for NFL players versus the general population. The other analyses comparing NFL players to the general population conducted by Lehman et al. (2012) focus on neurodegenerative causes of death. Several disease-specific results reported by Lehman et al. show a significant *increased* mortality risk for NFL players versus the US general population. This is the case for all neurodegenerative causes combined, as well as for two specific neurodegenerative diseases: amyotrophic lateral sclerosis (ALS) and dementia/ Alzheimer's disease (AD). Briefly, NFL players' risk for all neurodegenerative causes combined is about three times higher than that of the US general population, and the risk of ALS and AD is about four times higher. In all, there are ten deaths for all neurodegenerative causes combined in the cohort of NFL players reported by Lehman et al., including two with AD, six with ALS, and two with Parkinson's disease.

This chapter examines the following potential risk-factor variables in a large cohort of NFL players who played in the league between 1960 and 1986: age, race, playing-time body mass index, birthplace, and player position. In addition, I examined the number of seasons played in the NFL as a possible risk factor. No previous studies have examined the role of birthplace or number of seasons played on mortality for former NFL players.

METHODS OF THIS STUDY
The following sections detail the methods I used in this study.

STUDY COHORT

This study examines the vital status (i.e., whether alive or dead) of every individual who played at least one regular-season game in the NFL between 1960 and 1986. It identifies this cohort based on NFL team rosters (Troan, NFL Team Rosters 1960–86) during the respective target seasons.

VITAL STATUS

Determining whether a player is alive or dead is based on a vital-status end date of August 10, 2015. Players in this cohort who were alive on this date ranged in age from fifty to ninety-five years. I obtained vital status information from two online sources: the Player Profile pages of the NFL website and the Player pages of the Pro-Football-Reference website. In all instances, the information on players' vital status is identical between these two websites. However, only the Pro-Football-Reference site includes the date of death for deceased players. I calculated age at death (among deceased players) based on date of death and date of birth. Cause of death is not available for this study. Therefore, all analyses conducted are based on all-cause mortality.

DEMOGRAPHICS

I obtained date of birth, height, weight, and number of seasons played from the Player Profile pages on the NFL website. I obtained height and weight for players based on the last year they played in the NFL. Date of birth, height, and weight are also available both at the NFL and Pro-Football-Reference websites, and the information between the two sites is virtually always identical.

YEAR OF BIRTH

Year of birth/age is singly the most important factor in predicting mortality and must be used as a stratification/control variable in all relevant analyses. I obtained players' year of birth based on their date of birth. I used the following (eight) years of birth categories in the analyses: 1919–29, 1930–34, 1935–39, 1940–44, 1945–49, 1950–54, 1955–59, and 1960–65.

Only one player was born as late as 1965. Depending on the analysis, the continuous form of year of birth (i.e., each year) could be used instead of the previous categories.

RACE

Individual NFL race data are generally not available publicly. This study uses a novel approach to identify the race of players in the study cohort. In 1988, before his death in 1993, Arthur Ashe Jr., the African American tennis champion, in collaboration with a number of African American sports historians and publishers, compiled three volumes called *A Hard Road to Glory*. Each volume includes the names of most African American who played football, baseball, or basketball at the professional level in the United States.

The first step in determining race for the players in this study made use of the names listed in Ashe's book. I began by taking a random sample of 400 players listed by Ashe who are in the study cohort in order to confirm that they are indeed African American. I did this based on pictures found on the Internet in conjunction with historical facts and computer runs. For example, any player who attended an all-Black college, was assumed to be African American. Using this approach, I was able to confirm that 360 of the 400 randomly selected players from Ashe's book were African American. For the remaining 40 players, there was insufficient information available to make a determination regarding their race. *None of the 360 players in the study cohort listed in Ashe's book were white.* Based on this analysis, all 2,345 players listed in Ashe's book who are in the study cohort are coded as African American. This left about 5,500 players who were in the cohort, but not listed in Ashe's book. I expected some African Americans were missed by Ashe, but that the large majority of the remaining 5,500+ players would be white. This was determined using a similar method to the one described above. There were several historical facts that could be used to help make this determination using the computer. For example, between 1960 and 1972, only five African American quarterbacks played during a regular season in the NFL. (Howard, 2014) After identifying these five men, all other quarterbacks in the study cohort who played in the league before 1972 were coded as white. Using several historical facts like these plus pictures found on the Internet, the race of about 82% of all players in the cohort not listed in Ashe's book were identified. Foreign-born, Hispanic, and all other players who could not be positively identified as African American or white were excluded from all race analyses.

PLAYING-TIME BODY MASS INDEX

I computed playing-time body mass index (PT-BMI) using the standard formula of dividing weight in kilograms by the square of height in meters for players' final season in the NFL. In addition, I calculated a categorical BMI variable using standard cutoffs (World Health Organization 2006) as follows: normal weight is a PT-BMI of 18.5 to less than 25; overweight PT-BMI is between 25 and less than 30; obese is greater than or equal to 30. None of the NFL players in this study's cohort have an underweight PT-BMI of 18.5 or less.

BIRTHPLACE

Players' birthplaces, including the state of birth, are also provided on the NFL and Pro-Football-Reference websites. A number of players in the study cohort were born outside of the United States. I used a total of five birthplaces, or birth regions, for this study. I placed all players born in the United States into one of four regions as defined by the US Census Bureau (2015): the Northeast, the Midwest, the South, and the West. A fifth category used in this chapter includes all foreign-born players.

POSITION

I obtained players' positions from the Pro-Football-Reference website. The NFL website divides all current and former NFL players into one of two categories: current or historical. The NFL website provides position data for current players but not historical ones. Individuals who played in the 1960s and early 1970s, especially, sometimes played more than a single position. Based on data collected in this study, more than half of all players, 51.7 percent, who began their careers between 1945 and 1959 played more than one position. In all, nearly one of every five players in the study cohort, or 18.8 percent, played more than one position during their NFL careers. Consequently, I created dummy variables (i.e., yes/no) for each NFL position that is identified. Hence, a player can be coded as playing more than a single position. I categorized each individual position variable into one of six categories, as follows: offensive linemen, offensive backs, receivers, defensive linemen, defensive backs, and kickers. Again, a player can be classified in more than one of these position categories. In previous chapters, I classified players into a single position or position category only. This is because those previous chapters focus on individuals who played in the NFL between 2010 and 2014. Those are years in which almost all players played a single position only.

Number of NFL Seasons Played

I determined the number of NFL regular seasons played based on information found on the NFL and Pro-Football-Reference websites. I created categories based on number of seasons played, as follows: one to two seasons played, three to five seasons played, six to nine seasons played, or ten-plus seasons played. Number of seasons played can be viewed as a kind of exposure-response variable—that is, exposure to playing in the NFL and its potential relationship to mortality.

Statistical Plan

This study has a single outcome variable, namely a player's vital status (whether alive or dead) on August 10, 2015, and several potential risk-factor variables: race, PT-BMI, birthplace, position, and number of seasons played in the NFL. Year of birth is a control or stratification variable. I broke down or adjusted all results in this chapter by year of birth. In addition, I used several other variables to help describe the cohort: age (if alive), age at death (if deceased), year and age in first NFL season played, and number of career seasons played in the league.

I provided frequency distributions for all categorical study variables and gave descriptive statistics (i.e., mean, standard deviation, and median) for all continuous variables. I broke down the percentage of players alive and those dead as of August 10, 2015, by each of the potential risk-factor variables. I broke down all of these analyses by year-of-birth category.

I used logistic regression with a player's vital status (i.e., alive or dead) as the outcome variable to identify risk factors for NFL player mortality. Logistic regression is a statistical procedure that can be used to predict a binary outcome, like being dead or alive. I evaluated the ability of one variable to predict mortality in this procedure while I controlled, or held constant, the other variables. I conducted logistic regressions for each of the risk-factor variables separately while controlling for actual year of birth (rather than year-of-birth categories). I used a final logistic regression to identify independent risk factors of mortality. I entered all potential risk-factor variables, plus year of birth, into this final model simultaneously. I removed from this analysis variables that do not predict mortality. The final model includes only variables that are significant predictors of mortality, controlling for the other variables. I provided adjusted odds ratios with 95 percent confidence intervals for all of the logistic regressions. An adjusted odds ratio of two for a variable like race, for example, would indicate a twofold, or doubled, increase in the risk of death in one race versus another, controlling for any other variables that have been entered, like year of birth.

Results
The following sections detail the results of the analysis.

Description of Cohort
A total of 7,709 individuals played at least one game during one or more NFL regular seasons between 1960 and 1986 and are included in this study (see table 10-1). A total of 1,184 players (15.4 percent) died by the vital-status end date of August 10, 2015. The mean and median age of deceased players at the time of their death is 60.5 and 62.7 years, respectively.

Players that were still alive on August 10, 2015, average 64.2 years of age, and the median is 63.2.

The mean year of birth for the cohort is 1949.5, and the median is 1950. A relatively small number of players were born between 1919 and 1929 (*n* = 79; 1 percent) and between 1930 and 1934 (*n* = 335; 4.4 percent). A total of 861 players (11.2 percent) were born between 1935 and 1939. A total of 1,124 (14.6 percent) and 1,475 (19.1 percent) players were born during the 1940–44 and 1955–59 periods, respectively. About 1,200 to 1,300, or 16 to 17 percent, of cohort players were born during the remaining intervals (1945–49, 1950–54, and 1960–65).

I was able to positively identify a total of 6,535 players as being either African American (n=2,914) or white (n=3,621). Within this sub-sample, the percentage of African American players increased dramatically based on year of birth from 12.3 percent and 13.3 percent in the 1919-1929 and 1930-1934 categories to 55.9 percent and 61.0 percent in the 1955-1959 and 1960-1965 categories. A very similar pattern of results was obtained for the first year played in the NFL and race. Because of all of the missing data on race, these results are estimates and should be interpreted with caution.

The average first year played in the NFL by the cohort is about 1973, and the average player's age at that time was twenty-three years.

The most common birthplace for the cohort is the Southern region of the United States, with more than 46 percent of all players being from the South. The next closest birthplace is the Midwest, with 21 percent, followed by the West (16.5 percent) and the Northeast (14.2 percent). Nearly 2 percent of the cohort were born in a foreign country. The birthplace is missing for sixty-three players.

One-third of the study cohort played defensive back. The next-most-common position category is offensive backs (21.0 percent), offensive linemen (18.2 percent), receivers (17.6 percent), and defensive linemen (15.3 percent). Just over 4 percent are kickers. Again, these percentages add up to more than 100 percent because a substantial number of individuals played more than a single position category.

Slightly more than one-third of all cohort members played in only one or two regular seasons. Just under 25 percent played three to five seasons, and another 25 percent played six to nine seasons. About 17 percent of the cohort played ten or more NFL regular seasons. The mean number of career seasons played in the NFL by the cohort is 5.3, with a median of four seasons.

MORTALITY RISK-FACTOR ANALYSIS

In every analysis conducted in this chapter, year of birth is significant as a correlate or predictor of mortality in the expected direction. Players born in more distal years (i.e., older players) are more likely to die than players born in more recent years.

MORTALITY AND PLAYING-TIME BODY MASS INDEX

The mean Playing-Time Body Mass Index (PT-BMI) for the entire cohort is 28.5, and the median is 28.4. Only 10.4 percent of the cohort had a normal BMI. A total of 4,536 (58.8 percent) and 2,374 (30.8 percent) players are classified as either overweight or obese, respectively.

Table 10-2 provides results for the number and percentage of NFL players in the cohort who were deceased by the vital-status end date, broken down by the three PT-BMI categories. These results are stratified by each of the year of birth categories. No clear-cut pattern emerges with respect to normal versus overweight PT-BMI players. NFL players with PT-BMIs in the obese range, however, have a higher percentage of death than both the normal and overweight groups within every year of birth category, with the exception of the oldest group, those born from 1919 to 1929. For example, among players who were born between 1945 and 1949, about 11 percent of the normal and overweight PT-BMI players have died, compared to 17.2 percent of the obese players.

In logistic regression analysis that controls for year of birth, obese PT-BMI players have a 46 percent increased risk of dying relative to normal PT-BMI individuals (adjusted odds ratio = 1.46; 95 percent CI = 1.1,

1.9). However, there is no significant difference between normal and over-weight PT-BMI players in the percentage of players who have died.

MORTALITY AND RACE

The results in this section are based on the sub-sample of 6,535 African American and white players in the study cohort whose race were positively identified. As shown in table 10-3, for six of the eight year-of-birth categories, the percentage of African Americans who are deceased is higher than the percentage of whites (significance not tested). Among players who were born between 1930 and 1934, the percentage of African Americans and whites who are dead is about 58.5 percent for both races. Of players born between 1945 and 1949, 16.5 percent of the African Americans are deceased, compared to 10.8 percent of the white players. I obtained a similar pattern of results for all other year-of-birth groupings with the exception of the group born between 1940 and 1944 where African Americans averaged 20.2% dead and whites averaged 21.3%.

The logistic regression analysis that controls for year of birth is significant with respect to race. African American players have about a 36 percent increased risk of dying relative to whites (adjusted odds ratio = 1.36; 95 percent CI = 1.2, 1.6).

MORTALITY AND BIRTHPLACE

The results in this section exclude 146 players who were born outside of the United States plus 63 individuals with missing data on place of birth. Table 10-4 shows that within the year-of-birth categories 1919–29, 1930–34, 1945–49, 1950–54 and 1955–59, players born in the southern part of the United States have higher death rates than the three other regions (significance not tested). Within two of the remaining three year-of-birth categories, 1935–39 and 1940–44, players born in the Northeast have the highest death rates. In other words, players in the South or Northeast have the highest death rates in seven of the eight year of birth categories.

In the logistic regression analysis that evaluates birthplace controlling for year of birth, the western region of the United States serves as the index reference group. Compared to players born in the West, individuals born in the Northeast (adjusted odds ratio = 1.4; 95 percent CI = 1.05, 1.8) and South (adjusted odds ratio = 1.6; 95 percent CI = 1.3, 1.9) have significantly elevated mortality risks.

Mortality and Position

Table 10-5 shows results for position category broken down by the year-of-birth groupings. Defensive linemen have the highest death rates in three of the eight year-of-birth categories, 1935–39, 1945–49 and 1950–54. Receivers have the lowest death rates in three of the eight year-of-birth categories, 1930–34, 1935–39 and 1950–54.

I entered each of the six player-position variables separately, along with year of birth, into six logistic regressions predicting mortality. Two positions, offensive linemen and defensive linemen are significant risk factors for dying with adjusted odds ratios of 1.2 and 1.3 respectively; receivers and defensive backs have significantly lower death rates (adjusted odds=0.8 and 0.9 respectively). The remaining two positions, offensive backs and kickers, were not significant.

Mortality and Number of Seasons Played in the NFL

As shown in table 10-6, for a number of year-of-birth categories, the lowest percentages of deceased players are among those who played one to two NFL seasons. This includes the three birth-year categories that have the largest numbers of players, 1945–49, 1950–54, and 1955–59. The most striking mortality differences in this regard are observed among players born between 1945 and 1949. The percentage of players who died having played one to two seasons is 7.7 during this period. Players in the other three categories of NFL seasons played have about double the risk of being deceased, averaging 16.5 percent, 15.9 percent, and 13.3 percent in players with three to five seasons, six to nine seasons, and ten-plus seasons played, respectively.

The logistic regression results also reveal a significant preventative effect on mortality when just one to two seasons are played in the NFL. Using this group of players as the index reference, the adjusted odds ratios are both 1.3 and significant in players with three to five seasons, and six to nine seasons respectively.

FINAL LOGISTIC REGRESSION MODEL PREDICTING MORTALITY

In order to identify significant *independent* predictors of mortality, all variables that are significant in the previous logistic regressions reported in this chapter are entered into a final model. This includes year of birth, born in the South, born in the Northeast, race, BMI, defensive backs, offensive linemen, receivers, defensive linemen and number of years played in the NFL. Non-significant variables are dropped from this model one at a time until only significant items remain. The variables that were significant in this final logistic regression are: year of birth (i.e., being older), three to five and six to nine years played in the NFL (versus 1-2 seasons played), born in the South, African American race, and obese BMI. Of note, none of the position variables are significant in this analysis. Also, overweight BMI and being born in the Northeast fail to remain significant.

DISCUSSION

Some of the significant predictors of mortality were expected. Nevertheless, they raise issues about disparities in the risk of mortality among key groups of NFL players.

RACE

The findings related to age and race do not come as a surprise. Briefly, older players, African American players, and obese PT-BMI players were more likely to be deceased by August 10, 2015. In general, the risk of all-cause death among African Americans is elevated by about 35 percent, which is consistent with previous general-population research (Satcher et al. 2005). For a variety of reasons, I am unable to test the risk of death in my cohort of NFL players versus the general population.

Despite the inability to identify the race of all players in the study cohort, the race results presented in this chapter are very consistent. Specifically, relative to white players, African Americans have a higher percentage of death in players within most year-of-birth ranges. Moreover, race remains significant in logistic regression analyses that control for BMI, birth year, and other important variables. Again, and sadly, these are the kinds of findings that have been reported in the general population many times, as well as in the limited NFL mortality literature. Given the novel method used to identify race in this study and the large amount of unknown races, all of these results must be interpreted with great caution. Nevertheless, the consistency of these results and the similarities with previously published papers helps to bolster confidence in the methods that were used. Additional work on improving these methods and confirming the races of all cohort members is ongoing.

PT-BMI

The BMI results reported in this chapter strictly apply to players' heights and weights recorded when they were playing their final years in the NFL. The consistency and magnitude of the PT-BMI results seem especially noteworthy because they are based on BMI measurements that could have been obtained decades earlier in players' lives. This may be due to the high correlation between the BMI levels of younger and older players. In other words, individuals with low or high BMIs as young-adult NFL players may continue to have similar low or high BMIs years later, as older adults. However, we have no way of knowing this for certain. Nevertheless, obese PT-BMI is a significant and very consistent predictor of mortality in this study, even in the absence of knowing players' later-life BMI levels. The adjusted odds ratios reported in this chapter indicate that an obese PT-BMI elevates the risk of death by about 46 to 53 percent in NFL players.

Another method of aggregating BMI levels divides the obese group into three groups: obese, class-one BMIs go from thirty to less than thirty-five; obese, class-two BMIs go from thirty-five to less than forty; and obese, class-three BMIs are above forty (World Health Organization 2006). Several researchers have reported incremental risks of death in the general population based on these obese BMI groups (Borrell and Samuel

2014). Therefore, I examined obese PT-BMIs more closely in post hoc analyses.

Ninety-six players with PT-BMIs are in the obese, class two or three groups in this study; however, only six players are in the latter group. I conducted a post hoc logistic regression to predict mortality for the following three PT-BMI groups while controlling for year of birth: (1) normal and overweight PT-BMIs combined (index reference); (2) obese, class-one BMIs; and (3) obese, class-two and -three PT-BMIs combined. Class-one obese players have an adjusted odds ratio of 1.4 in this analysis, which is significant. The adjusted odds ratio for class-two/-three obese players is 5.6 (95 percent CI = 3.2, 9.9), indicating that this group has more than five times the risk of dying compared to the normal PT-BMI players. This is easily the largest adjusted or unadjusted odds ratio uncovered in this study.

Body size and shape tend to change with age, and lifestyle can play a role in the nature of these changes. Specifically, after age thirty, lean tissue can be lost, and the amount of body fat may increase. Individuals could gain a third more body fat relative to when they were younger. Even height can diminish over time at the rate of about a centimeter every ten years after forty years of age. The pace of height loss can accelerate after age seventy (US National Library of Medicine 2014; Minaker 2011; Shah and Villareal 2010). With respect to weight, males will generally gain weight up until the age of fifty-five but may lose some of this as they get older (US National Library of Medicine 2014; Minaker 2011; Shah and Villareal 2010). Again, I have no way of knowing whether PT-BMI is correlated with BMI later in life within the cohort studied in this chapter. The study results, however, definitely do not allow us to rule this out as a possibility.

Position

Player position is not a meaningful predictor of mortality in this study. When I added the other study variables to the final logistic regression, none of the position variables remained significant. Player position is correlated with some of the other variables studied in this chapter. For example, some positions are played mainly by African Americans, and some positions include players with higher BMIs. When I controlled PT-BMI, race, and other study variables in the final logistic regression, player position is not significant.

Baron and colleagues (2012) report that CVD risk of death is significantly increased for defensive linemen versus other positions. The coding the NIOSH researchers use for player position fails to recognize that many individuals played multiple positions during the study period. As noted earlier, more than half of the players who began their careers between 1945 and 1959 played more than a single position. Not taking this into account could impact study results. In any case, there is no explanation in any of the three NIOSH mortality publications regarding how individuals who play multiple positions are handled in the analysis.

BIRTHPLACE

Place of birth and its relationship to mortality have been studied extensively for the US general population. Before this study, however, place of birth and its relationship to mortality was not examined among NFL players. This study indicates that NFL players born in the southern region of the United States have about a 40–60 percent increase in their risk of dying. As noted earlier, the nine states with the highest death rates in the country are all located in the South (Centers for Disease Control 2014). Hence, the fact that NFL players born in the South also have an elevated risk of mortality may not come as a surprise. However, this study has now provided some indication of the magnitude of this effect among NFL players for the first time. Moreover, this result remains significant when year of birth, race, PT-BMI, and several other critical variables are controlled in the analysis. I would describe these findings with respect to mortality and being born in the South as consistent and robust.

These birthplace results are especially concerning given the number of NFL players who are born in the South. About 46 percent of NFL players in this study cohort were born in this region, and this could currently be as high as 50–55 percent (Kacsmar 2013). In 2010, about 37 percent of the US population was born in the South (US Census Bureau, 2010), so this group's representation in the NFL clearly exceeds its numbers in the general population.

NUMBER OF NFL SEASONS PLAYED

The findings related to mortality and the number of seasons played are novel and interesting. These results seem especially noteworthy because the NIOSH researchers never reported the intersection of these two factors. In fact, the 2012 NIOSH studies exclude players with less than five years of credited service in the NFL. Clearly, in the current study, the group of players with just one to two seasons of NFL experience have a significantly lower risk of mortality than the other three groups. However, there is no sign whatsoever of the risk of death rising incrementally as individuals play more and more NFL seasons. There are similar percentages of deceased players among the three groups of players who have played three to five, six to nine, and ten-plus seasons. In other words, players with six to nine seasons played do not have higher death rates than individuals with three to five years. If anything, the logistic regression results indicate that the group of players with ten-plus seasons played has a slightly lower risk of dying than the two other groups with more than two seasons played.

CONCLUDING REMARKS

Age as a risk factor for mortality is a fact of life. Even though life expectancy has increased in virtually all countries over time, with few exceptions death rates still increase with age. There is, however, nothing "binding" about some of the other risk factors identified in this chapter. While expected, and consistent with previous findings on the general population and the NFL, there is a difference between African Americans and whites on mortality and between individuals born in the South versus other regions of the United States, which would not be the case in a "fair world." The Healthy People 2010 program defines a number of health-related objectives the United States hoped to accomplish during the first ten years of the twenty-first century. One of the program's two stated goals was to eliminate health disparities (Healthy People 2010). This program has now been extended through 2020. As the Healthy People 2020 website notes, disparities in health do not only refer to racial or ethnic disparities. "If a health outcome is seen to a greater or lesser extent between populations, there is a disparity" (Healthy People.gov 2015). This study has documented significant and consistent differences in the risk of mortality between African Americans and whites, as well as between players born in the South versus other regions of the United States. These disparities appear to be the same ones that exist between groups of people in the general population. These are not issues that will be resolved rapidly, but they do need to be addressed. Unlike race and birthplace, which are fixed and essentially out of an individual's control, BMI is something that, at least in part, can be viewed as a personal responsibility. In some cases, obesity begins in childhood and continues throughout life. As one researcher notes, "Childhood obesity is associated with an increased risk for other diseases, not only during youth but also later in life, including diabetes, arterial hypertension, coronary artery disease, and fatty liver disease" (Barton 2012).

In addition to the individual taking responsibility, there are a number of groups and organizations that can help people avoid or eliminate obesity. Speaking specifically about childhood obesity, the Centers for Disease Control (2011) states, "Opportunities are available at multiple levels—communities, schools, industry, media, families, and individuals—to reduce the prevalence of obesity." Most, if not all, of these opportunities apply to adults as well. For playing in the NFL, certain positions, particularly offensive linemen, require that players be large in size. Many offensive linemen in the NFL currently weigh more than 300, or even 350 pounds, and being lighter could result in a competitive disadvantage.

Moreover, once a player reaches a weight like this, it could be more difficult to lose the weight in later years. Playing-time BMI is a consistent risk factor for mortality in the NIOSH studies, as well as this study. This risk appears to apply to obese, rather than overweight, BMIs, and increases dramatically in the highest grades of BMI obesity (i.e., classes two and three). The NFL and NFLPA should consider developing weight-reduction programs, if they do not exist already, for retired players with BMIs in the obese range.

The NIOSH studies consistently show a decreased risk of death among NFL players versus the general population. Nevertheless, mortality issues still are greater for select groups of players. While the current study does not address this topic, these kinds of effects could be prevalent in other levels of football, and possibly even in other sports. It is, in fact, unlikely that mortality risk factors among NFL players are very different from other groups of people outside of the league.

The current generation of NFL players is obviously different from the cohort studied in this chapter. Some of the recent demographic trends, however, may not bode well for mortality risk in current players. There is evidence that the number of players in the league with one or more of the risk factors for mortality documented in this chapter is increasing over time. This is likely to be the case with respect to the number of African American players, individuals born in Southern states, and players with PT-BMIs in the obese range. See table 1-1 in chapter 1. The mean and median body weight, for example, in the 2010–14 cohort of players are about 245 and 240 pounds, respectively. This compares to a mean and median body weight of 221 and 220 pounds in the players in the 1960–86 mortality cohort studied in this chapter. Assuming that the risk factors for mortality are about the same now as they were in the 1960–86 cohort, there could be a growing number of current players who may be at risk for mortality in future years. We cannot afford to wait another twenty to forty years to begin to study whether or not being African American, being obese according to BMI, and being born in a Southern state will continue to be risk factors for mortality in current NFL players, and more broadly, in the general population.

REFERENCES

Ashe, A. R. Jr. 1993. *A Hard Road to Glory: Football.* New York: Harper Collins.

Baron, S. L. M. J. Hein, E. Lehman, and C. M. Gersic. 2012. "Body Mass Index, Playing Position, Race and the Cardiovascular Mortality of Retired Professional Football Players." *American Journal of Cardiology* 109: 889–96.

Barton, M. 2012. "Childhood Obesity: A Life-Long Health Risk." *Acta Pharmacologica Sinica* 33 (2):189–93.

Berrington de Gonzalez, A., P. Hartge, J. R. Cerhan, et al. 2010. "Body-Mass Index and Mortality among 1.46 Million White Adults." *New England Journal of Medicine* 363(23): 2211–9.

Borrell, L. N. and L. Samuel. 2014. "Body Mass Index Categories and Mortality Risk in US Adults: The Effect of Overweight and Obesity on Advancing Death." *American Journal of Public Health.* 104 (3): 512–9. http://www.ncbi.nlm.nih.gov/pubmed/24432921.

Centers for Disease Control and Prevention, Division of Reproductive Health. 2015. "Infant Mortality." http://www.cdc.gov/reproductivehe alth/MaternalInfantHealth/InfantMortality.htm.

Centers for Disease Control and Prevention, National Center for Health Statistics. 2012. "Mortality in the United States." http://www.cdc.gov/ nchs/data/databriefs/db168.htm.

Centers for Disease Control and Prevention. National Center for Health Statistics. 2014. *National Vital Statistics Report* 64 (2), table 19.

Department of Health and Human Services. Healthy People 2010: Understanding and Improving Health, 2nd ed., Washington, DC: Government Printing Office, 2000.

Flegal, K. M., M. D. Carroll, C. L. Ogden, and L. R. Curtin. 2010. "Prevalence and Trends in Obesity among US Adults, 1999–2008." *Journal of American Medical Association* 303 (3): 235–41.

Fletcher, M. A. 2013. "Research Ties Economic Inequality to Gap in Life Expectancy." *Washington Post*, March 10.

Healthy People. 2010. "Health People Goals." http://www.healthypeople.gov/2010/About/goals.htm.

Healthy People.gov, Office of Disease Prevention and Health Promotion. "Disparities." http://www.cdc.gov/nchs/healthy_people/hp2020.htm.

Howard, G. 2014. "The Big Book of Black Quarterbacks" *Deadspin*. http://deadspin.com/the-big-book-of-black-quarterbacks-1517763742.

Kacsmar, S. 2013. "Where Does NFL Talent Come From?" *Bleacher Report*. http://bleacherreport.com/articles/1641528-where-does-nfl-talent-come-from.

Lehman, E. J., M. J. Hein, S. L. Baron, and C. M. Gersic. 2012. "Neurodegenerative Causes of Death among Retired National Football League Players." *Neurology* 79 (19): 1970–74.

Minaker, K. L. "Common Clinical Sequelae of Aging." In *Goldman's Cecil Medicine*, 24th ed., edited by L. Goldman and A. I. Schafer. Philadelphia: Elsevier Saunders, 2011.

National Institute for Occupational Safety and Health. "Letter to the National Football League Players Association (NFLPA) written to Mr. Frank Woschitz on January 10, 1994." Centers for Disease Control and Prevention. HETA 88-085. http://www.cdc.gov/niosh/hhe/reports/pdfs/1988-0085-letter.pdf.

NFL. "Player Profiles." http://www.nfl.com/players.

Ogden, C. L., M. D. Carroll, L. R. Curtin, et al. 2006. "Prevalence of Overweight and Obesity in the United States, 1999–2004." *Journal of the American Medical Association* 295:1549–55.

Phillips, M., K. Ryan, and J. Raczynski. 2011. "Public Policy versus Individual Rights in Childhood Obesity Interventions: Perspectives from the Arkansas Experience With Act 1220 of 2003" Centers for Disease Control and Prevention. *Preventing Chronic Disease* 8 (5). http://www.cdc.gov/pcd/issues/2011/sep/10_0286.htm.

Pro-Football Reference.com. "Players." http://www.pro-football-reference.com/players/.

Robert Wood Johnson Foundation. "MetroMap: New Orleans, Louisiana, June 19, 2013." http://www.rwjf.org/en/library/infographics/new-orleans-map.html.

Satcher, D., J. R. Fryer., G. E. McCann, J et al. 2005. "What If We Were Equal? A Comparison of the Black-White Mortality Gap in 1960 and 2000." Health Affairs. http://content.healthaffairs.org/content/24/2/459.full.

Schubauer-Berigan, M. K., M. J. Heim, W. M. Raudabaugh, et al. 2011. "Update of the NIOSH Life Table Analysis System: A Person-Years Analysis Program for the Windows Computing Environment." *American Journal of Industrial Medicine* 54: 915–24.

Shah, K., and D. T. Villareal. "Obesity." In *Brocklehurst's Textbook of Geriatric Medicine and Gerontology*, 7th ed., edited by H. M. Fillit and K. Rockwood. Philadelphia: Elsevier Saunders: 2010.

Troan, J. "NFL Team Rosters, 1960–1986." JT-SW.com. http://www.jt-sw.com/football/pro/rosters.nsf.

Mihoces, G. 2014. "Annual Diversity Report Give NFL 'B' For Racial, Gender Hiring Practices." *USA Today* Sports, September 17. http://www.usatoday.com/story/sports/nfl/2014/09/17/racial-and-gender-report-card-grade-b-diverstiy/15780865/.

US Census Bureau. 2015. "Census Regions and Divisions of the United States." http://www2.census.gov/geo/pdfs/maps-data/maps/reference/us_regdiv.pdf.

US Census Bureau. 1990–2010. "Census 2010; Census 2000; 1990 Census." InfoPlease, U.S. Population by Region. http://www.infoplease.com/ipa/A0764220.html.

US National Library of Medicine. "Aging Changes in Body Shape." Last modified October 27, 2014. https://www.nlm.nih.gov/medlineplus/ency/article/003998.htm.

Wong, M. D., M. F. Shapiro, J. Boscardin, and S. L. Ettner. 2002. "Contribution of Major Diseases to Disparities in Mortality." *New England Journal of Medicine* 347 (20). http://www.nejm.org/doi/pdf/10.1056/NEJMsa012979.

Woolf, S. H., R. E. Johnson, G. E. Fryer Jr., G. Rust, and D. Satcher. 2004. "The Health Impact of Resolving Racial Disparities: An Analysis of US Mortality Data." *American Journal of Public Health*. 94 (12): 2078–81.

World Health Organization. 2006. "BMI Classification." http://apps.who. int/bmi/index.jsp?introPage=intro_3.html.

————. 2015. "Life Expectancy Data by Country, Global Health Observatory Data." http://apps.who.int/gho/data/view.main.680.

Table 10.1. Background and Vital Status Characteristics of 1960–86 Cohort of NFL Players				
Vital Status on August 10, 2015				
Alive or Dead	N	%		
Alive	6,525	84.6%		
Dead	1,184	15.4%		
*Race^^*	N	%		
African American	2,914	44.6%		
White	3,621	55.4%		
	N	Mean	SD	Median
Playing-Time Body Mass Index	7,709	28.5	2.9	28.4
BMI Categories	N	%		
Normal (18.5 - < 25)	799	10.4%		
Overweight (25 - < 30)	4,536	58.8%		
Obese (> 30)	2,374	30.8%		
Birthplace				
Foreign / Outside of US	146	1.9%		
Midwest	1,609	21.0%		
Northeast	1,087	14.2%		
South	3,540	46.3%		
West	1,264	16.5%		
Missing (n=63)				
Six-Group Position*				
Offensive back	1,618	21.0%		
Offensive line	1,405	18.2%		
Receiver	1,359	17.6%		
Defensive line	1,181	15.3%		
Defensive back	2,544	33.0%		
Kicker	338	4.4%		

Table 10.1. Background and Vital Status Characteristics of 1960–86 Cohort of NFL Players (Continued)					
	N	%			
Number Seasons Played in the NFL					
1–2	2,584	33.5%			
3–5	1,895	24.6%			
6–9	1,919	24.9%			
10+	1,311	17.0%			
Other Variables	N	Mean	SD	Median	
Year of birth	7,710	1949.5	9	1950	
Age (if alive)	6,525	64.2	8.3	63.3	
Age at death (if dead)	1,170^	60.4	13.8	62.7	
Year of first NFL season played	7,709	1972.6	8.9	1973	
Age at first NFL season played	7,709	23.1	1.3	23	
Number of NFL seasons played	7,709	5.3	4	4	

*Some individuals played two or more positions. Hence, numbers and percentages sum to more than the number of players and to more than 100%.

^ 14 players who died with missing data on age at death   ^^Includes 6,535 players whose race was identified

	Table 10-2. Mortality among NFL Players (1960–86) by Playing Time Body Mass Index and Year of Birth							
	Year of Birth							
	1919–29	1930–34	1935–39	1940–44	1945–49	1950–54	1955–59	1960–65
Playing Time Body Mass Index								
Normal PT-BMI								
N Alive	1	13	50	80	118	144	158	127
N Dead	9	21	21	23	14	11	6	3
Total N	10	34	71	103	132	155	164	130
% Dead	90.0%	61.8%	29.6%	22.3%	10.6%	7.1%	3.7%	2.3%
Overweight PT-BMI								
N Alive	13	90	355	550	683	771	790	634
N Dead	33	112	186	118	84	58	37	22
Total N	46	202	541	668	767	829	827	656
% Dead	71.7%	55.5%	34.4%	17.7%	11.0%	7.0%	4.5%	3.4%
Obese PT-BMI								
N Alive	7	34	151	261	289	316	450	440
N Dead	16	65	98	92	60	36	34	25
Total N	23	99	249	353	349	352	484	465
% Dead	69.6%	65.7%	39.4%	26.1%	17.2%	10.2%	7.0%	5.4%

	Table 10-3. Mortality among NFL Players (1960–86) by Race^ and Year of Birth							
	Year of Birth							
	1919–29	1930–34	1935–39	1940–44	1945–49	1950–54	1955–59	1960–65
Race								
African American								
N Alive	1	17	102	241	404	521	639	613
N Dead	8	24	64	61	80	59	50	30
Total N	9	41	166	302	484	580	689	643
% Dead	88.9%	58.5%	38.6%	20.2%	16.5%	10.2%	7.3%	4.7%
White								
N Alive	18	111	367	498	519	526	525	397
N Dead	46	157	191	135	63	34	19	15
Total N	64	268	558	633	582	560	544	412
% Dead	71.9%	58.6%	34.2%	21.3%	10.8%	6.1%	3.5%	3.6%
^^Includes 6,535 players whose race was identified								

	Table 10-4. Mortality among NFL Players (1960–86) by Birthplace^ and Year of Birth							
	Year of Birth							
	1919–29	1930–34	1935–39	1940–44	1945–49	1950–54	1955–59	1960–65
Birthplace								
Midwest								
N Alive	6	38	136	203	243	259	281	207
N Dead	10	47	58	44	27	22	12	16
Total N	16	85	194	247	270	281	293	223
% Dead	62.5%	55.3%	29.9%	17.8%	10.0%	7.8%	4.1%	7.2%
Northeast								
N Alive	4	26	88	134	145	168	166	165
N Dead	13	38	59	42	18	8	10	3
Total N	17	64	147	176	163	176	176	168
% Dead	76.5%	59.4%	40.1%	23.9%	11.0%	4.6%	5.7%	1.8%
South								
N Alive	6	51	229	408	492	576	636	554
N Dead	24	79	143	117	100	61	43	21
Total N	30	130	372	525	592	637	679	575
% Dead	80.0%	60.8%	38.4%	22.3%	16.9%	9.6%	6.3%	3.7%
West								
N Alive	4	19	77	116	186	208	280	234
N Dead	9	30	32	26	10	12	11	10
Total N	13	49	109	142	196	220	291	244
% Dead	69.2%	61.2%	29.4%	18.3%	4.6%	5.5%	3.8%	4.1%
^ Excludes 146 players born outside of the US								

	Table 10-5. Mortality among NFL Players (1960–86) by Position* and Year of Birth							
	Year of Birth							
	1919–29	1930–34	1935–39	1940–44	1945–49	1950–54	1955–59	1960–65
Six-Group Position								
Offensive back								
N Alive	7	40	152	180	225	274	243	208
N Dead	20	52	77	64	29	23	17	7
Total N	27	92	229	244	254	297	260	215
% Dead	74.1%	56.5%	33.6%	26.2%	11.4%	7.7%	6.5%	3.3%
Offensive line								
N Alive	7	39	124	167	185	191	226	187
N Dead	19	61	76	51	31	13	16	12
Total N	26	100	200	218	216	204	242	199
% Dead	73.1%	61.0%	38.0%	23.4%	14.4%	6.4%	6.6%	6.0%
Receiver								
N Alive	2	29	95	151	196	213	268	231
N Dead	12	32	42	32	27	14	7	8
Total N	14	61	137	183	223	227	275	239
% Dead	85.7%	52.5%	30.7%	17.5%	12.1%	6.2%	2.6%	3.4%

	Table 10-5. Mortality among NFL Players (1960–86) by Position* and Year of Birth (Continued)							
	Year of Birth							
	1919–29	1930–34	1935–39	1940–44	1945–49	1950–54	1955–59	1960–65
Defensive line								
N Alive	8	32	86	143	164	153	196	151
N Dead	18	45	61	48	35	20	13	8
Total N	26	77	147	191	199	173	209	159
% Dead	69.2%	58.4%	41.5%	25.1%	17.6%	11.6%	6.2%	5.0%
Defensive back								
N Alive	5	55	187	311	347	405	459	407
N Dead	22	71	100	58	45	32	25	15
Total N	27	126	287	369	392	437	484	422
% Dead	81.5%	56.3%	34.8%	15.7%	11.5%	7.3%	5.2%	3.6%
Kicker								
N Alive	2	4	30	46	51	45	60	45
N Dead	4	6	17	10	8	7	1	2
Total N	6	10	47	56	59	52	61	47
% Dead	66.7%	60.0%	36.2%	17.9%	13.6%	13.5%	1.6%	4.3%

* Some players played more than one position.

Table 10-6. Mortality among NFL Players (1960–86) by Number Seasons Played in the NFL and Year of Birth								
	Year of Birth							
	1919–29	1930–34	1935–39	1940–44	1945–49	1950–54	1955–59	1960–65
Number Seasons Played in NFL								
1–2 Seasons								
N Alive	2	30	210	326	419	421	455	385
N Dead	0	36	109	84	35	31	22	19
Total N	2	66	319	410	454	452	477	404
% Dead	0.0%	54.5%	34.2%	20.5%	7.7%	6.9%	4.6%	4.7%
3–5 Seasons								
N Alive	1	26	118	206	273	307	359	320
N Dead	9	39	67	52	54	29	23	12
Total N	10	65	185	258	327	336	382	332
% Dead	90.0%	60.0%	36.2%	20.2%	16.5%	8.6%	6.0%	3.6%
6–9 Seasons								
N Alive	9	35	131	210	228	320	383	285
N Dead	13	70	79	51	43	29	22	11
Total N	22	105	210	261	271	349	405	296
% Dead	59.1%	66.7%	37.6%	19.5%	15.9%	8.3%	5.4%	3.7%
10+ Seasons								
N Alive	9	46	97	149	170	183	201	211
N Dead	36	53	50	46	26	16	10	8
Total N	45	99	147	195	196	199	211	219
% Dead	80.0%	53.5%	34.0%	23.6%	13.3%	8.0%	4.7%	3.7%

Epilogue

• • •

I'VE BEEN WAITING TO WRITE this chapter for more than five years now. After spending hundreds of hours identifying data sources, creating databases, cleaning data, analyzing data, interpreting results, and writing two books, I'm going to drop my scientific facade and talk to you as a fellow football fan. While I'll speak from the heart, I'm going to attempt to keep in mind the results reported in this book. There will, however, be times in this chapter when I go beyond the science with some of my thoughts, feelings, and beliefs.

I began this book by saying that I love football. Nobody, including a guy like Daniel J. Flynn, will ever tell me otherwise. I hate to honor his book *The War on Football* (2013) by citing and quoting him, so I'll keep this brief. Here's the first paragraph on Flynn's book cover: "From concussion doctors pushing 'science' that benefits their hidden business interests to lawyers clamoring for billion-dollar settlements in scam litigation, America's game has become so big that everybody wants a cut. And those chasing the dollars show themselves more than willing to trash a great sport in hot pursuit of a buck" (Flynn 2013, inside book cover).

I'm sure that Flynn doesn't even know who I am and that his comments are directed at others. In reality, there are going to be some people who try to make money in nefarious ways related to the "health and well-being" of professional football players. How low can some people go? Nevertheless, I take Flynn's comments and his entire book personally.

My own intent is not to trash football, and the idea of making money on this work is ludicrous. Is there really something wrong with identifying some significant problems with the hope of improving things in the future? Isn't this what many people do when they really care about something? I'd just like to see safer football played by individuals who don't end up in jail or dead.

I must admit, however, that I can't stand to watch a bunch of immature, maladjusted, spoiled, rich, out-of-control player brat stars competing on NFL fields every Sunday (and Monday, and Thursday, and several Saturdays) during the football season. While I know that individuals like this exist, they represent a small minority of all NFL players. It would be relatively easy for me, or someone else, to write a book about all of the good and charitable things that many NFL players do. There are actually dozens of NFL players serving their communities in meaningful ways and "giving back" to others who are less fortunate (NFL/Community ongoing).

Unfortunately, most of what's written nowadays about the NFL focuses on negative aspects of the game, and this book is no exception in this regard. What sets this book apart is that it's based on original empirical research that "doesn't take sides." It probably surprised many readers to learn that NFL players have lower DUI rates than comparably aged males in the general population. To steal from an old sports adage, "That's why they play the games," or in the case of DUI, why the empirical analyses have to be done. Obviously, however, the DUI findings reported in this book are not cause for players or league officials to be spiking a bottle of Jack Daniels in an NFL end zone. In fact, considerably more attention is required before DUI, domestic violence, and so many other violent and nonviolent crimes committed by NFL players can be considered anything close to being "fixed."

Here are several final thoughts and ideas about some of the findings contained in this book.

ARRESTS

Four chapters in this book focus on arrests of NFL players, and I've noted numerous times that there is a presumption of innocence for arrestees in the United States. Unfortunately, some of the arrested players will be, or already have been, convicted of crimes. Depending on the charges and circumstances, jail time can follow. I can't provide any kind of estimate of the number of NFL players who have served, or currently are serving, time in jail. However, I'm sorry to report that several former players are currently serving life sentences, and others are serving time that will almost certainly last the remainder of their lives.

Some sports-related websites have published a range of racy lists related to NFL players serving time in prison. Here are several examples: "Top Ten NFL Prison Sentences" (Bleacher Report 2009); "The NFL All-Prison Team" (Bleacher Report 2012); "Hall of Shame: Eleven NFL Players Who Went to Jail" (Sporty Insider 2013); and "The Fifteen Worst Crimes Committed by NFL Players" (ArrestRecords.com n.d.). While sometimes interesting, these types of articles fail to provide quantifiable material that could better serve to impart knowledge. (As I've documented in this book, the authors of these types of articles and other well-intended sports pieces related to crime and arrests in the NFL are not exactly the world's leading epidemiologists.) Nevertheless, articles like these do tell us that there are more than a few former NFL players who have been jailed. Moreover, some of this jail time is related to convictions for extremely serious crimes, including murder, rape, manslaughter, and domestic violence.

Jail time has to be considered one of the ultimate forms of "lost seasons." Even probation, or simply being charged with a crime, can draw shame and embarrassment to a player, as well as unfavorable public attention from fans, teammates, opponents, coaches, owners, and many others. Most Americans can be forgiving and tend to believe in giving second chances. Remarkably, many have somehow even forgiven the NFL star convicted on federal and state charges of running a dog-fighting gambling rink and shooting, electrocuting, and hanging dogs (Animal Legal

Defense Fund 2011). Tolerance, however, can wane as crimes become more heinous and victims more innocent. NFL player perpetrators who show little or no remorse can rapidly work their way onto thousands of shit lists across the country.

The victims of the crimes committed by NFL players can experience far-reaching losses. In extreme instances, victims are killed or maimed. In other circumstances, victims spend time in hospitals, are disabled, and may carry with them significant psychological scars that haunt them for the rest of their lives. Moreover, it's not just the individuals who are directly victimized by crimes; it's also their family members and loved ones.

Following his conviction in 2015, and just before being sentenced to life without parole for the murder of a twenty-seven-year old man, a former NFL star listened to the impact statement of the victim's sobbing mother: "The day I laid my son, Odin, to rest, I think my heart stopped beating for a moment. I felt like I wanted to go into that hole with my son" (Ursula Ward, quoted in *Daily News* 2015).

It was clear from a number of similar statements given by family members of the victim that they had been totally devastated by their loss. To make matters worse, this same former NFL star has yet to stand trial for an altogether-separate double murder that authorities believe he committed in Boston.

Besides in regard to DUI, the chapters on arrest in this book have not included direct comparisons with the general population. For most of the crimes examined in this book, there's no way to really know whether arrest rates of NFL players are higher or lower than for the general population. However, the temporal trends in arrest rates among NFL players versus the general population are the most disconcerting. Clearly, over time, arrest rates among NFL players for numerous offenses have been going in the opposite direction than national trends, where there are declining rates for some of the most serious and violent types of offenses. This raises a big red flag for me. Until all or most of these rates for NFL players show improvement on a consistent basis, over a prolonged period of time, there will continue to be cause for concern.

Suspensions and Physical Fines

Some of these infractions involve the most violent, illegal hits in the game. In fact, victims of these offenses can sometimes be sidelined for weeks and months with serious injuries directly related to these incidents. Victims' seasons and even careers can be jeopardized by these often intentional and reckless acts. Fines, rather than suspensions, are often meted out to the players who commit these acts. When the league issues suspensions for on-field violent acts, they tend to be only a few games in length. We now know, from chapter 7, that fines for physical offenses represent only a small fraction of players' salaries. In general, the fines and suspensions given for on-field illegal violence are insufficient given the severity of some of these incidents. In a week-six game in 2014, for example, one player was fined a measly $25,000 for "unsportsmanlike conduct" when, according to one report, he "took an opponent's ankle, twisted it hard, and tried to break it with his bare hands—twice, to different players" (Grossman 2015).

I firmly believe that intentional, illegal, violent on-field acts resulting in an injury, and perhaps lost playing time to an opponent, require much more severe punishments than "slap-on-the-wrist" fines and short suspensions. Repeat offenders should be suspended for more than a couple of games, and if warranted, an entire season. Playing in the NFL does not entitle players to viciously assault an opponent. The punishments for such offenses need to be reasonable but also proportionate to the respective infractions.

There also seems to be a fair amount of the league "sanitizing" some of these violent incidents. Is it really sufficient and appropriate to officially call the offense described in the previous paragraph "unsportsmanlike conduct"? If we were to be more accurate, this act should be called an "assault." That's what it would be called in any court of law in the United States. If I twisted and attempted to break a fellow worker's ankle, I'd be fired instantly, and criminal, plus civil, charges would probably follow. Assaults are assaults, on or off an NFL playing field. There's enough violence in the NFL when players stick to the rules.

CAREER CHAOS

There's far-more career craziness in the NFL than this book has described. In addition, the chaos doesn't end with getting cut or retiring (Holstein 2015), and it can continue throughout a former player's lifetime. Each season now starts with a ninety-man roster at the beginning of training camp in July. By opening day, usually around the first week of September, only fifty-three men remain on each team roster. More than 40 percent of the players are cut and gone within about two months of training camp. Some of these players may appear on practice squads or take vacated roster spots during the regular season. Many of them attempt to make an NFL team in the years that follow. Most, however, will probably just disappear from the face of the professional football world.

The situation for players who make an opening-day roster isn't exactly clear-cut, either. Based on my own 2010–14 data, less than 40 percent of these individuals will participate in all sixteen regular games during the regular seasons that they play. We saw in chapter 9 that nearly one of every four individuals drafted in 2010 played only one or two of the next five regular seasons. We also saw how the number of years played in the league is related to players' placement in the draft, with the players drafted earlier playing more seasons than later-round draft picks. Even going back to the 1960–86 cohort of players described in chapter 10, about one-third of the players played only one or two seasons in the league.

According to the NFLPA and others, the average length of an NFL player's career is just 3.3 years (Holstein 2015; Ninomiya 2015). The NFL apparently has a different methodology for calculating the career length of players and somehow comes up with about 6.8 years. All indications are that the NFLPA estimate is much closer to reality in this case (Bennett 2011).

Not only are average NFL careers short; rookie contracts are far less lucrative than they were before the 2011 Collective Bargaining Agreement. As one author explains, "Each *pick* has a predetermined amount…[A] player and his agent know the exact dollar figures the moment he is drafted. They also know the length; every contract is for four years…As for salaries, the vast majority of drafted players have four years of nonguaranteed minimum salaries" (Brandt 2014).

Only signing-bonus money is really guaranteed in the NFL. According to one Internet writer, "The rest of the contract is completely subject to player performance and injury avoidance" (Porter 2012). Signing bonuses for players just drafted are keyed to one's placement in the draft and are generally added to the minimum mandated salary for rookies—about $420,000 currently. Players selected in the fourth round, about the middle of the draft, currently get signing bonuses in the half-million-dollar range (Spotrac 2015). When base salaries and signing bonuses are added together, this seems like a decent chunk of change. But again, the player has to make it through the years of his contract, and performance and injury issues can often interfere.

With careers lasting a little more than an average of three years, this first NFL contract could also be the last for a significant percentage of players. A substantial number of players will not even make it to the end of their first contract. Once they're out of the NFL, other professional football options are quite limited. The Canadian Football League or the Arena Football League may work for a few players, but most will just be out of a job and not too happy about it. As one author puts it, "In light of what we know about the experiential uncertainty of the end of playing days, and given the face-saving quality of saying one 'retired,' versus admitting to being 'cut' or 'fired,' it's safe to say that a relatively small minority of players leave the game happily of their own accord" (Holstein, Jones, and Koonce 2015, 93).

MORTALITY

The mortality results presented in this book are fascinating, yet troubling, especially with respect to obese players, those born in the South, and African American players. In conjunction with the American Public Health Association, the United Health Foundation has published annual state-health indicator rankings since 1990. This is a "state-by-state analysis of factors affecting the health of individuals and communities across America" (United Health Foundation 2015, 2). The following is a partial list of health indicators published in 2015, *where Southern states have all five of the worst ratings relative to all other states in the country*: smoking, obesity, physical inactivity, children in poverty, low-birth-weight babies, preventable hospitalizations, diabetes, poor mental-health days, poor physical-health days, infant mortality, cardiovascular deaths, cancer deaths, premature deaths, and a number of other illnesses (United Health Foundation 2015). There are actually dozens of more published health indicators in which Southern states fare worse than most other states in the United States (National Center for Health Statistics ongoing).

Findings in this book reveal that there are more domestic-violence arrests, more suspensions for substance abuse, and a higher risk of mortality among players born in Southern states. In the case of mortality, these findings are evident even when factors like race, age, and playing-time BMI are taken into account. At the same time, the number and proportion of NFL players born in Southern states has been increasing over time. Unofficially, about 50 to 55 percent of current NFL players were born in the South (Kacsmar 2013), which is considerably higher than the percentage of the US population born in these states, at about 37 percent in 2010 (US Census Bureau 2010). The following is a chart containing the states within each of the four US regions.

With the South faring so poorly on so many health indicators, and more and more NFL players born in this region of the country, a "perfect storm" could be developing. Although it is unlikely that there is a direct cause-and-effect relationship between any of these health indicators and the actions and behaviors of NFL players, some of the players could be growing up in environments where the roots of malcontent, crime, and ill health have already been planted in them. It would probably take great effort on the part of these players to overcome the odds and alter the course of some of the potential negative outcomes they are likely to confront in later years.

States within Each US Region Based on US Bureau of the Census*	
Region	*State*
Midwest	Indiana, Illinois, Michigan, Ohio, Wisconsin, Iowa, Kansas, Minnesota, Missouri, Nebraska, North Dakota, South Dakota
Northeast	Connecticut, Maine, Massachusetts, New Hampshire, Rhode Island, Vermont, New Jersey, New York, Pennsylvania
South	Delaware, District of Columbia, Florida, Georgia, Maryland, North Carolina, South Carolina, Virginia, West Virginia, Alabama, Kentucky, Mississippi, Tennessee, Arkansas, Louisiana, Oklahoma, Texas
West	Arizona, Colorado, Idaho, New Mexico, Montana, Utah, Nevada, Wyoming, Alaska, California, Hawaii, Oregon, Washington

Source: US Census Bureau, "Census Bureau Regions and Divisions with State FIPS Codes," http://www2.census.gov/geo/pdfs/maps-data/maps/reference/us_regdiv.pdf accessed 2015.

I doubt that the league would develop interventions specifically for retired players born in the South. By all accounts, however, these players do require special attention related to a range of arrest and mortality outcomes. The same risks can be said to exist among African Americans, although the empirical data presented in this book have found only a connection between race and mortality. Other possible associations could not be assessed due to the unavailability of data on race for 2010–14 players. There is some limited evidence linking race to some of the arrest outcomes presented, but this is strictly indirect based on possible relationships between playing position and race. Much more research on this is required.

The focus on the elimination of health disparities, as advocated by the Healthy People Initiatives of 2000 and 2010, must be taken more seriously by the NFL. This would definitely include health disparities related to being African American, being obese, and being born in a Southern state. All three of these factors are statistically significant independent risk factors for mortality among NFL players.

Some of the playing-time BMI results reported in this book are especially interesting and worthy of follow-up research. About 90 percent of the NFL players studied in this chapter have PT-BMIs that are in the overweight range and higher. Nearly 59 percent of the cohort is in the overweight BMI category, and another 31 percent are obese. In general, being obese appears to be an American epidemic. This condition may also be widespread on a worldwide basis, as is sometimes called "globesity." Flegal and colleagues (2010) report that 63.5 percent of the US general population of males between twenty and thirty-nine years of age are overweight or obese. More than 27 percent of the general population of males in this same age range fall into the obese category.

Looking to the Future

While this book focuses on NFL players, some of the findings may now, or at some point in the future, be relevant to players at other levels of football. The NFL may help to "set the bar" in many respects for some of the other levels of the sport. While there are currently fewer than two thousand NFL regular-season players each year, there are well over a million younger athletes playing college and high school football. In 2012–13, nearly 1.1 million high school football players in the United States were playing for more than fourteen thousand high school teams (National Federation of State High School Associations, cited in CNSnews.com 2014).

Improvements in NFL policies, procedures, and protocols have the potential to trickle down to other levels of football. However, a lack of money, particularly in high school sports, can make it difficult to incorporate some of the safeguards and standards that are part of every NFL game. One *New York Times* report discusses the problem of medical resources in high school football games this way: "According to the National Athletic Trainers' Association, only 42 percent of high schools in the United States have access to a certified athletic trainer, let alone a physician, during games or practices. In some poorer rural communities, concussed players are taken to doctors with no experience with head injuries. Youth leagues with players as young as eight and nine rarely, if ever, have any medical personnel on hand; when a child is hurt, a parent, assuming one is present, walks out on the field, scoops up the child, and carries him or her off" (Schwarz 2010).

In contrast, up to twenty-seven medical personnel man every NFL game these days (Siebert 2013).

A number of on-field deaths, primarily due to traumatic head injuries, occur among high school football players each year (Mueller and Cantu 2011). The same generally does not occur in the NFL (Miller 2013). Certainly, there are many more at-risk players at the high school level, but the resources available to effectively manage serious on-field injuries could be lacking (Schwarz 2010). In the absence of adequate medical personnel at games played by tens of thousands of American boys and young men, there is the potential for real disaster here. In my opinion, any school or organization that can't afford to have adequate medical staff at football games should just close down their football programs. Some high schools have already done this (Hoatson 2015). As one Internet writer notes, "Nationally, participation in high school football has declined, and an increasing number of football programs have been terminated due to lack of interest, excessive injuries, or parents' decisions not to allow their boys to play. Will the trend toward elimination of high school football continue?" (Hoatson 2015).

While the NFL continues to boom, there are, indeed, some disconcerting trends related to young people and playing football. According to one Bloomberg poll, "Fifty percent of Americans say they wouldn't want their son to play the sport, and only 17 percent believe it'll grow in popularity in the next twenty years" (Bloomberg Politics 2014). A 2014 Internet article titled "Nine NFL Players Who Won't Allow Their Sons to Play

Football" presents the views of several former and current NFL stars who have strong positions on their own children not playing football. Even President Obama has weighed in publicly on the topic, saying, "I would not let my son play pro football" (Obama, quoted in the *Huffington Post* 2014). Parents, in large numbers, are dissuading their kids from playing football (Lavigne 2012). A public-opinion poll conducted by ESPN Reports states that 57 percent of a thousand parents surveyed "said that recent stories about the increase in concussions in football have made them less likely to allow their sons to play in youth leagues" (Lavigne 2012).

When I wrote my first book about three years ago on the epidemiology of concussions in the NFL, I called it *Pigskin Crossroads*. I felt that the concussion crisis and the ongoing large class-action lawsuit had the potential to put the league out of business. About a week after that book was released, an agreement was reached that seemed to "end the crisis." The initial settlement of about $765 million (Brinson 2014) was later revised to an uncapped amount to "ensure funds are available to any eligible retired player who develops a compensable injury" (NFL 2014).

In the aftermath of the concussion settlement, the NFL has remained intact, and players continue to get concussions. In fact, the NFL's revenue was about $12 billion in 2014, up 16 percent from the previous season, and is expected to rise another billion this year (Isidore 2015). Moreover, and unofficially, concussions increased dramatically during the 2015 regular season compared to the previous five years. (Markowitz 2016, unpublished data) Nevertheless, the crossroads I'd written a book about seemed to fade, dissipate, and all but disappear.

I don't believe any of the issues or problems documented in this book have affected the league to the extent that concussions have. This may be because concussions occur on the playing field, while arrests and deaths (later in life) do not. Concussions are considered a direct "side effect" of the game itself, while illegal acts off of the playing field are not. Collectively, the dozens of incidents on and off the playing field may be putting the

NFL at yet another critical crossroads. It seems as if the league and its players are constantly teetering on the brink of disaster on the one hand and achieving unprecedented profit and success on the other. It's this ongoing tension and uncertainty between such disparate outcomes that generally set the league and its players apart on so many levels.

REFERENCES

Animal Legal Defense Fund, Winning the Case against Cruelty. 2011. "Animal Fighting Case Study: Michael Vick." http://aldf.org/resources/laws-cases/animal-fighting-case-study-michael-vick/.

ArrestRecords.com. n.d. "The 15 Worst Crimes Committed by NFL Players." http://www.arrestrecords.com/the-15-worst-crimes-committed-by-nfl-players.

Ashe, A. R. Jr. 1993. *A Hard Road to Glory: Football.* New York: Harper Collins.

Baron, S. L., M. J. Hein, E. Lehman, and C. M. Gersic. 2012. "Body Mass Index, Playing Position, Race and the Cardiovascular Mortality of Retired Professional Football Players." *American Journal of Cardiology* 109: 889–96.

Belson, K. 2014. "Goodell's Pay of $44.2 Million in 2012 Puts Him in the Big Leagues." *New York Times,* February 14. http://www.nytimes.com/2014/02/15/sports/football/goodell-nfl-commissioner-earned-44-2-million-in-2012.html?_r=0.

Bennett, D. 2011. "The NFL's Official Spin on Average Career Length Is a Joke." *Business Insider,* April 18. http://www.businessinsider.com/nfls-spin-average-career-length-2011-4.

Bloomberg Politics. 2014. "Half of Americans Don't Want Their Sons Playing Football, Poll Shows." http://www.bloomberg.com/politics/articles/2014-12-10/bloomberg-politics-poll-half-of-americans-dont-want-their-sons-playing-football.

Brinson, W. 2014. "Judge Rejects Initial $765m NFL Concussion Lawsuit Settlement." http://www.cbssports.com/nfl/eye-on-football/24409040/judge-rejects-initial-765m-nfl-concussion-lawsuit-settlement.

Flegal, K. M., M. D. Carroll, C. L. Ogden, L. R. Curtin. 2010. "Prevalence and Trends in Obesity Among US Adults, 1999–2008." *Journal of American Medical Association* 303 (3): 235–241.

Grossman, E. 2015. "Why Marshawn Lynch Tops the List of the Most Fined in the NFL." *Men's Journal*, January 26. http://www.mensjournal.com/adventure/races-sports/why-marshawn-lynch-tops-the-list-of-the-most-fined-in-the-nfl-20150126.

Hoatson, R. M. 2015. "High School Football Has Become Too Dangerous." http://www.nj.com/opinion/index.ssf/2015/10/high_school_football_has_become_too_dangerous_opin.html.

Holstein, J. A., R. S. Jones, and G. E. Koonce Jr. 2015. "Is There Life after Football? Surviving the NFL" New York: New York University Press.

Isidore, C. 2015. "NFL Revenue: Here Comes Another Record Season." CNN Money, September 10. http://money.cnn.com/2015/09/10/news/companies/nfl-revenue-profits/index.html.

J., Matt. 2009. *Bleacher Report*. "Top 10 NFL Prison Sentences." http://bleacherreport.com/articles/215328-top-10-nfl-prison-sentences.

Kacsmar, S. 2013. "Where Does NFL Talent Come From? *Bleacher Report*. http://bleacherreport.com/articles/1641528-where-does-nfl-talent-come-from.

Lavigne, P. 2012. "Concussion News Worries Parents." http://espn.go.com/espn/otl/story/_/id/8297366/espn-survey-finds-news-coverage-concussions-leads-majority-parents-less-likely-allow-sons-play-youth-football-leagues.

Longo, Ralph. 2012. *Bleacher Report*. "The NFL All-Prison Team." http://bleacherreport.com/articles/1014955-the-nfl-all-time-prison-team.

Markowitz, J. Unpublished data. "Concussion incidence in the NFL, 2010-2015."

Miller, J. 2013. "Stone Johnson Died 50 Years Ago from Injury in NFL Game." *USA Today* online, August 31. http://www.usatoday.com/story/sports/nfl/2013/08/29/nfl-player-death-anniversary-stone-johnson-len-dawson-chiefs/2735393/.

Mueller, F. O., and R. C. Cantu. 2011. "Football Fatalities and Catastrophic Injuries, 1931–2008." Durham, NC: Carolina Academic Press.

National Center for Health Statistics, Health Indicators Warehouse. http://www.healthindicators.gov/.

National Federation of State High School Associations, quoted in CNSNEWS.com. 2014. "Football is Top Sport in U.S.: 1,088,158 High School Players." February 2. http://www.cnsnews.com/news/article/terence-p-jeffrey/football-top-sport-us-1088158-high-school-players.

NFL. n.d. "Community." http://www.nfl.com/community.

————. 2014. "Revised Settlement in Concussion Suit Reached: Funds Uncapped." http://www.nfl.com/news/story/0ap2000000361552/article/revised-settlement-in-concussion-suit-reached-funds-uncapped.

Ninomiya, K. 2015. "How Long Is the Average Career of an NFL Player?" Livestrong.com, May 4. http://www.livestrong.com/article/15527-long-average-career-nfl-player/.

Obama, Barack, quoted in Mollie Reilly. 2014. "Obama on Concussions: I Would Not Let My Son Play Pro Football." *Huffington Post*, January 19. http://www.huffingtonpost.com/2014/01/19/obama-nfl-concussions_n_4627866.html.

Schwarz, A. 2010. "Eagles' Handling of Head Injury Draws Spotlight," *New York Times*, September 15. http://www.nytimes.com/2010/09/16/sports/football/16concussions.html?_r=2&scp=1&sq=rhode%20island%20trainers&st=cse.

Siebert, D. 2013. "What Is Medical Care Like on an NFL Sideline?" *Bleacher Report*. http://bleacherreport.com/articles/1850732-what-is-medical-care-like-on-an-nfl-sideline.

Spotrac. 2015. "NFL 2015 Draft Tracker." http://www.spotrac.com/nfl/draft/.

Sporty Insider. "Hall of Shame: 11 NFL Players Who Went to Jail" http://www.sportyinsider.com/hall-of-shame-8-nfl-players-who-went to jail/2013.

US Census Bureau. 1990–2010., "US Population by Region, 1990–2010" http://www.infoplease.com/ipa/A0764220.html.

Ward, Ursula. 2015. "Mom of Odin Lloyd Still Aches, But Finds Forgiveness for Killer Aaron Hernandez." *Daily News*, April 15. http://www.nydailynews.com/sports/football/mom-odin-lloyd-aches-finds-forgiveness-article-1.2186561.

World Health Organization. 2006. "BMI Classification." http://apps.who.int/bmi/index.jsp?introPage=intro_3.html.

www.ingramcontent.com/pod-product-compliance
Lightning Source LLC
LaVergne TN
LVHW051046080426
835508LV00019B/1726